DOES IT MATTER
WHAT
YOU
BELIEVE?

ELVIN C. MYERS

WestBow
PRESS®
A DIVISION OF THOMAS NELSON
& ZONDERVAN

CONTENTS

ACKNOWLEDGMENTS

I am indebted to the following individuals for their help with advice, with proofreading the text, and with the preparation of the manuscript: Derek Conklin, Karen Conklin, Linda Bedore, Lynne Thomas, and my wife, Ann Myers, who helped with the preparation of the text and provided loads of encouragement. My heartfelt thanks to each one.

PREFACE

The purpose of this book is to answer the many questions about what the Bible teaches and how it differs from other belief systems. Does it really matter what we believe? People have said that we are all climbing up the same mountain and eventually will arrive at the same place at the top; we are just taking different routes to get there. After reading the Bible for seventy-five years, however, I can confirm that no such mountain has ever been found in the scriptures. That mountain is a myth and a dangerous one. "Sometimes a way seems right, but the end of it leads to death" (Proverbs 14:12, 16:25).

The sole authority for my beliefs is based wholly on the Bible, never on tradition. "All scripture is inspired by God and is useful for teaching, for refutation, for correction, and for training in righteousness" (2 Timothy 3:16). God is the sole instructor. He uses the Bible to teach us everything we need to know to be saved from everlasting judgment and to live in eternity with Him. Scriptures quoted in this text are entirely from The *New American Bible.*

Not a word of this book has been written to offend, but rather, to explain and to cause one to think and ask, Do I believe the truth that will save my soul from a fearful, never-ending judgment? Do I even know the truth? There is no time to learn like the present. The Bible, which God inspired to be written, tells us what to believe. It should be the sole authority of every believer.

INTRODUCTION

The truth has never been popular. The first chapter of Paul's epistle to the Roman church records this as a fact of history.

> The wrath of God is indeed being revealed from heaven against every impiety and wickedness of those who suppress the truth by their wickedness. For what can be known about God is evident to them, because God made it evident to them. Ever since the creation of the world, his invisible attributes of eternal power and divinity have been able to be understood and perceived in what he has made. As a result, they have no excuse; for although they knew God they did not accord him glory as God or give him thanks. Instead, they became vain in their reasoning, and their senseless minds were darkened. While claiming to be wise, they became fools and exchanged the glory of the immortal God for the likeness of an image of mortal man or of birds or of four-legged animals or of snakes. Therefore, God handed them over to impurity through the lusts of their hearts for the mutual degradation of their bodies. They exchanged the truth of God for a lie and revered and worshiped the creature rather than the creator, who is blessed forever. Amen. (Romans 1:18–25)

Reading carefully, we note that the people who are referenced here "knew God" (Romans 1:21). They knew the truth, but they deliberately exchanged the truth for a lie. The verses in Romans 1 say they did this because they did not like to retain God in their minds; they declared their independence from Him. Who were these people? They were the early civilizations who populated the earth. The belief systems they created persist to this day. There is nothing new under the sun. Nothing has changed. God's truth is still rejected today, and ancient lies persist.

So, just asking, where do you stand? Do you know the truth? Do you believe the truth? If you believe the truths that God has made known to us, then welcome to the minority of believers in the world today. By divine inspiration, Matthew wrote the following words in his gospel: "Enter through the narrow gate; for the gate is wide and the road broad that leads to destruction, and those who enter through it are many. How narrow the gate and constricted the road that leads to life. And those who find it are few" (Matthew 7:13–14).

It's a fact. The road, the way, the belief system that leads a human soul home and into the presence of God is not crowded. There are few who find it; it has been that way from the start. Are you on the right road? Are you one of the few?

This book was written to steer people away from errors that might damn their souls. It is my hope that what is written here will lead people away from the never-ending judgment of hell and the lake of fire that is mentioned in Revelation 20:14–15, a place where the soul never dies.

Many people who know the truth never speak up. They are afraid to point the way out of wrong thinking to those who are in error. There is too much fear of rejection, fear of offending, fear of losing friendships, and fear of ridicule. It hurts to be rejected. Sometimes, we are afraid that we won't be persuasive enough, and we fear not having sufficient knowledge to convince people.

But, dear reader and friend, way too much is at stake to remain silent. Whether people will admit it or not, those who do not know the truth are dependent upon those who do. And those who know the truth are responsible for making the truth known. We must speak up. This book is my attempt to speak up.

It is the plan of this book to show how people in the Bible, who would be considered deeply religious today, were rejected by God and never entered His presence when they died. They await judgment. It is necessary to show the extreme danger in trusting tradition.

The material here sets forth doctrinal issues, showing what the Bible teaches and what it does not. The Bible is our sole guide because it is God's Word and not mankind's. Every word in the original writings of the Bible was dictated to those who wrote it. They never once added to or subtracted from it. This inspired Word of God was protected by God's power down through the centuries, guarding it from sabotage. It is as much God's Word today, in our English language, as it was in the original Hebrew, Aramaic, and Greek it was written.

Paul reminds his coworker and pastor friend Timothy that "All scripture is inspired by God and is useful for teaching, for refutation, for correction, and for training in righteousness, so that one who belongs to God may be competent, equipped for every good work" (2 Timothy 3:16–17). What a blessing it is to have in our possession our very own copies of God's inspired and preserved Word in our own languages. What a wonderful provision God has made for us.

On January 5, 1975, at 9:27 p.m., a ship carrying ore struck the Tasman Bridge in Australia, causing the bridge to collapse. The falling bridge sank the ship. Four cars, carrying five motorists, went over the edge of the broken bridge, and people fell to their deaths before traffic was stopped.

Reader's Digest carried the account of a man who nearly became a victim himself.[1] He was heading home that evening, following a bus that was a short distance ahead. The taillights of the bus

---

[1] S. Johnson, "Over the Edge," *Reader's Digest*, November 1977.

disappeared, so the man pulled over to the side of the road, walked up to the bridge, and discovered what had happened: the bridge had collapsed. Looking back, he saw another car approaching and frantically waved his arms to stop the driver. The driver barely stopped in time, his front wheels dangling over the edge of the broken bridge. Between them, these two drivers stopped oncoming traffic, thus averting further tragedy.

Reader, do you think the first man was right to warn oncoming motorists of the bridge, thus saving them from the peril of those who did not know about the collapse? Was it the right thing to do? This book is the waving arms to those who are in danger of eternal peril for their lack of knowledge or for believing in the wrong things. Consider them carefully.

CHAPTER 1
IT MATTERED WHAT SOME BELIEVED

YOU HAVE HEARD of people referred to as being deeply religious. The Bible refers to people like this often, and what it says is not pleasant. You have probably heard it said that it doesn't matter what you believe if you are sincere and without hypocrisy. The argument goes something like this: I'm just as good as you are. If you are going to heaven, so am I. God loves me just as much as He loves you. A God of love would never send a soul to hell. There are many ways to heaven, and my way is just as good as yours. No one is perfect in what he or she believes; neither can anyone be, for to err is human. God does not expect us to be perfect. What we believe is not important. God accepts us just as we are.

In God's eyes, there is a sense in which one person is just as good as another. But being good does not assure one that he or she is bound for heaven. There is a sin problem that must be dealt with. They say it is seriously wrong to think that God would judge a sinner and cast him or her into hell and the lake of fire. The Bible says, "Just as it is appointed that human beings die once, and after this the judgment" (Hebrews 9:27). That Bible verse alone is enough to tell us that there is judgment to come, but there are also many other

Bible verses that say the same thing. God will be the judge. He will judge people on the decisions they made during their lifetimes.

Admittedly, our knowledge is incomplete. How incomplete? How much do we need to know to escape the judgment of God? Where is the authority we can appeal to and learn from about what to believe and about whether what we know is correct?

Assuming and believing that there is a God, He is the authority on all matters of faith and conduct. If anyone in the universe knows, God knows. If anyone knows how to make truth known and easy to understand, it is God. God has done exactly this by putting the truth in writing, so we appeal to the Bible—the holy scriptures and the Word of God. If God can create the universe, the planet Earth, and all that's on it, it should be an easy thing for God to author the Bible by inspiration and to protect it from error. It would be easy for God to breathe the exact words and precise thoughts He wants us to know and believe into the minds of chosen people. In the Bible, we learn whether it matters to God what we believe. What an easy way to make truth known: have it written down and put it in black and white. This is what the Bible says about itself. There is a gold mine of information in 2 Timothy 3:16–17. First, it is implied that the scriptures are the source of wisdom—God's wisdom. He shares His wisdom with us in the scriptures. "Which are capable of giving you wisdom for salvation through faith in Christ Jesus" (2 Timothy 3:15). Note that the verse does not say *faith in religion, the church,* or *good works*; neither does it depend on following what the preacher, priest, seminary professor, or TV evangelist says. It is God in His Word who tells us how to be saved from the "wages of sin" (Romans 6:23).

II Timothy 3:16 tells us plainly that all scripture is inspired by God. *Inspire* means "to breathe into." Into what did God breathe His words? He breathed them into the minds of those who were chosen to write them down. How much did these chosen people write down? The verse says *all scripture*. How much is all? Does all mean some, most, much, or nearly everything, or does it mean 100 percent? *All* means absolutely everything, so what was originally written by inspiration were all God's words, and they have never been anything more or anything less.

Third, 2 Timothy 3:16 tells us that God's revealed Word is profitable to us for four important things. *Profitable* means beneficial. The four beneficial things are teaching (doctrine we must believe), refutation (rebuke, rejection of unacceptable behavior), correction (correcting our erring beliefs), and training in righteousness (telling us how to live righteously).

Belief is no guessing game. God tells us what to believe, and we must believe what He says. We all need refutation, to be reproved. We need to know what God censures and what is unacceptable to Him. What God condemns and what the consequences are for disobedience and unbelief is no secret. It is crucial that we know what conduct God expects of us. Since it is written down in black and white and is accessible to us, we are without excuse if we do not know the truth. We do not like to be reproved, but reproof is necessary.

The next thing that profits us is correction. As sinners, the easiest thing in the world is to stray from the path set forth in the Bible. We get lots of help in straying into the unbelieving world. False teaching and a rebellious nature makes corrections necessary. Sin is attractive and alluring. The wrong way leads to death, even if the way seems good and right. It may seem good and right to us, but it is not acceptable to God.

Finally, we need instruction in righteousness. We need to know what it is and how we get it. We do not have any righteousness of our own that is acceptable to God. God says, "There is no one just, not one" (Romans 3:10). Then how do we become righteous? When a sinner makes the decision to obey God and receive the gift of everlasting life by believing in the Lord, Jesus Christ, for salvation, God then freely confers righteousness upon that person. Righteousness is a gift. Righteousness leads to right thinking and right behavior. We cannot stand in God's presence without being righteous.

Second Timothy 3:17 teaches us that the four things we learned in 2 Timothy 3:16 profit those who are of God and those who belong to God. The writers of the Bible were men of God. Paul and Timothy were men of God furnished unto all good works. *Furnished* is a nautical term. When a ship was about to embark on a sea voyage, it was made fit for the journey. By experience, the captain of the ship knew exactly what it would take to travel from one point to another. A sufficient amount of supplies would be taken on board to last the entire trip. There had to be enough food and drinking water, repair parts, and sails or fuel to deliver the cargo. When everything was on board, the ship was completely furnished to make a safe and successful journey. By the same token, people of God must be properly furnished for ordinary daily life and for ministry. He or she is furnished by the scriptures with doctrine, reproof, correction, and instruction in righteousness for the journey through life and ministry.

There are numerous examples in the Bible of people who were deeply religious. They believed in God, followed a worship system, did good works, and yet were rejected by God because they believed the wrong things. It is extremely important for us to know this so that we don't fall into the same error. Nothing but the truth will make a sinner free from the penalty of sin. We must not substitute religion or Christian philosophy for biblical doctrine. Second Timothy was written by Paul to a preacher. Timothy was instructed to "Be eager to present yourself as acceptable to God, a workman who causes no disgrace, imparting the word of truth without deviation" (2 Timothy 2:15). He could have God's approval only if he taught God's Word correctly. His hearers could be saved only if they were correctly taught. Salvation is never accidental. Failure to teach the Word of God correctly may result, first, in souls being lost for eternity. Second, the teacher will suffer a loss of rewards for his or her labor.

Third, it will result in insufficient knowledge for the hearers of the Word. This is no small matter.

In 2 Timothy 2:16, erroneous theology was labeled as profane and was to be avoided; idle talk for such people will become more and more godless. Verse seventeen says that wrong beliefs spread like gangrene. Does this sound like it matters what we believe? It's a fact of life that nobody's perfect, neither in behavior nor in belief. To err is definitely human. Error must be minimized.

We know that God hates hypocrisy, and we should too. Even so, being as right as we can be in what we believe is of the highest importance. Precision in our beliefs comes from making every effort to restrict our beliefs to a very narrow set of doctrines. We enter a relationship with God through a narrow gate. The broader gate welcomes all kinds of beliefs, but this may lead a sinner to everlasting destruction. Matthew says, "Enter through the narrow gate [of beliefs], for the gate is wide and the road broad that leads to destruction, and those who enter through it are many. How narrow the gate and constricted the road that leads to life. And those who find it are few" (Matthew 7:13–14). We should never apologize for being narrow-minded. We owe it to ourselves to ask: Which road am I walking on? Am I one of the few, or am I going with the majority in what they erroneously believe?

Deeply Religious People in the Bible Who Erred

Cain

At the beginning of the Bible, we have an example of a deeply religious man named Cain. He was the first child born to humans and the eldest son of Adam and Eve. There is no doubt that Cain believed in God. God spoke to Cain, and Cain responded; they talked with each other. Cain and his younger brother, Abel, knew God's will, learning it either directly from God or from their parents. The brothers knew the same things. They were born with a sinful nature that spiritually separated them from God, but God made a way for them to be reconciled to a relationship with Him. God made the rules. There was only one way that called for belief and obedience. There was no ignorance, no lack of knowledge or misunderstanding, and no excuse for not knowing God's way.

Genesis 4 tells us that Cain brought an offering to God. Being a "tiller of the ground" (Genesis 4:2), he brought the first harvest to the Lord as an offering. Amazingly, God rejected Cain's offering. Abel also brought an offering to the Lord. He was a shepherd and brought a lamb, which he killed and then sprinkled its blood on the altar.

God accepted Abel's offering. It is of the highest importance that we know the reason. One offering was brought in faith, in accordance with God's requirements; the other was brought without faith and was not what God required. Cain's offering was from the ground that God had cursed. When Adam and Eve sinned against God and disobeyed Him, God took away the coats of fig leaves they had made to cover their nakedness and provided coats of animal skins for them instead. To do this, it was necessary to sacrifice lambs to provide the coats of skin. The lesson was that, in order to stand in God's presence and be spiritually united with Him, they had to do what God did: namely, sacrifice a lamb. The lamb would portray the Lord, Jesus Christ, of whom John the Baptist would say, "Behold, the Lamb of God, who takes away the sin of the world" (John 1:29). Abel saw the need for a sacrificial, blood-sprinkled offering, but Cain either saw no such need, or just simply refused to offer one. This is known in the Bible as "the way of Cain" (Jude 1:11).

Cain's actions mark the beginning of religion in humanity. Religion is the invention or creation of new beliefs that humans fashion out of their own minds. The mind of God was set aside in favor of the mind of Cain. Since it comes from the minds of humans, religion takes all kinds of forms and practices. So, when people ask why there are so many belief systems in the world today, there's the answer. It began with Cain and branched out into an assortment of different beliefs. Christianity is different. It is based on the Bible and does not depart from it.

How can a sinner be washed and made clean in the sight of God and be made free from the wages of sin? Only by believing in the finished work of the Lord, Jesus Christ. There is no other way for a sinner to be saved. By faith and obedience, Abel's sins were covered by the blood of the lamb that he sacrificed; Cain's sin remained. He brought an offering, but not a sacrifice or blood. He felt no need of being cleansed from sin. God spoke to him directly about the matter and gave him an opportunity to repent and turn to Him. Cain refused. Instead, the Bible says, "Cain than left the Lord's presence and settled in the land of Nod, east of Eden" (Genesis 4:16).

What a sad ending for a deeply religious man. He was a God-believing man, but as far as the record shows, Cain was disobedient to the end and never changed his mind. What shall we make of this? Did it matter what Cain believed? It mattered altogether. It cost him his soul for eternity. He is forever lost and doomed to never-ending torment. What a terrible fate for someone who could so easily have been saved from divine judgment.

How good of the Lord to inspire the book of Genesis to include such an important truth. We must believe God, rather than humanity, and obey His Word rather than trusting religions. Never trust in the fruit of the land like Cain did. Our good works do not impress God enough to save us. By inspiration, Paul wrote, "For the wages of sin is death [separation from God], but the gift of God is eternal life in Christ Jesus our Lord" (Romans 6:23). Like all gifts, His offer of salvation must be received. God saves and gives everlasting life only to those who chose to believe His Word about salvation through Jesus Christ and who trust in His blood to cleanse them from sin. Have you trusted in the Lord, Jesus Christ, to save you? Do you know if you have everlasting life?

Korah

Who was Korah? He was a citizen of Israel. He was born in Egypt before the Exodus and had the privilege of crossing the Red Sea with his people. He journeyed through the wilderness and witnessed the power of God's deliverance, guidance, and daily provisions. The leader, who God appointed to lead Israel out of Egypt and through the wilderness, was Moses. God gave Moses His Word, which, according to Bible scholars, contains 613 laws that Israel was expected to obey completely. The Israelites did not have to make up a belief system; in fact, they were forbidden to do so. God told them what to believe.

Korah was a Levite. He was of the priestly tribe of Israel; his ancestry could be traced back to Levi, the son of Jacob, through Israel's carefully kept genealogical records. Not much is said about Korah, but we know he was a member of the nation that God created to have a people for His name. Korah believed in God.

In Numbers 16, we read the account in which Korah was the leader of 250 people who rebelled against Moses. "Holding an assembly against Moses and Aaron, they said, 'You go too far! The whole community, all of them, are holy; the Lord is in their midst. Why then should you set yourselves over the Lord's assembly?'" (Numbers 16:3). Korah was the leader of those in Israel who refused to recognize that Moses was God's appointed leader and that Moses had God's Word for the people. They accused Moses and Aaron of assuming power of leadership for themselves. In doing so, Korah and friends rejected God's appointed leader and His Word. They set about to establish their own beliefs and ways of worship. It cannot be emphasized too strongly how dangerous such an action is, as Korah and company were to find out. God does not tolerate rejection and interference. His error was remembered in the New Testament and referred to as "the rebellion of Korah" (Jude 1:11).

Numbers 16:29–35 shares how God dealt with the matter of Korah's rebellion. In summary of these verses, Moses called Israel's attention to Korah's rebellion. There was something God wanted

His people to see. Moses said that if Korah died a natural death, it would prove that Korah was right and that he and his brother, Aaron, were totally out of order. But, if the earth opened up and swallowed Korah and some of the men who had followed him, it would prove that Korah was wrong and that God had indeed chosen Moses to lead Israel and give them His Word.

So, what happened? The Bible says the earth opened up and swallowed Korah and many of the men who followed him. Of the rest of the men who followed Korah and were not swallowed up, fire came down from heaven and devoured them all. It was God who cleaved the earth and sent the fire as He judged those who rebelled. This is what Moses wanted Israel to see. Did it matter what Korah and his followers believed? It mattered very much. It cost those in rebellion their very souls for time and eternity.

New Testament Religious People Who Erred

An example of deeply religious people who will perish forever into the darkness and torment of hell are mentioned in Matthew's gospel. The Lord said, "Not everyone who says to me, 'Lord, Lord,' will enter the kingdom of heaven, but only the one who does the will of my Father in heaven. Many will say to me on that day, 'Lord, Lord, did we not prophesy in your name? Did we not drive out demons in your name? Did we not do mighty deeds in your name?'" The Lord will say, "'I never knew you. Depart from me, you evildoers'" (Matthew 7:21–23).

Who are these deeply religious people the Lord called evil doers? They believed in the Lord, did many good works, cast out demons, and evangelized the masses, all in the name of the Lord. Why would they be cast out into darkness? The passage refers to a future judgment that will take place at the Lord's Second Coming. They will be judged because good works are not saviors. God wants people to do good works, but only for the sake of service and not for salvation. Their judgment is related to what they believed. Their works were good, but their doctrines were incorrect. They invented religious beliefs and added them to what the scriptures say. When people believe things that are not found in the Bible, those beliefs stand the highest chance of being wrong. Continuing to believe wrong things may cost a person his or her soul. God will reject these religious people forever and cast them into darkness and never-ending torment. Who are these people? They are those who, today and in the future, believe and teach false doctrines rather than truth. Do you think it matters what a person believes?

The Pharisees and Rabbis

The elders in Israel were the religious leaders of God's earthly people. They were self-appointed; God did not appoint them. They claimed to be followers of Moses by whom God gave the law to Israel. At times, they obeyed the law, but at other times, they did not. Among the elders were the rabbis, scribes, and Pharisees. The rabbis had their beginning back in the days when Israel was returning from seventy years of exile in Babylon. The priesthood barely functioned in teaching Israel God's laws, so the rabbis appointed themselves as the nation's teachers and spiritual leaders. At first, they were good teachers; but as time went by, they distanced themselves from the Mosaic law and began to make up their own religious ideas. They passed these ideas off as God's teachings, and by the time the Lord began His ministry in Israel, the rabbis had set aside the scriptures in favor of their own teachings. Their teachings became known as the traditions of the fathers or elders. The Lord rebuked them and said, "You disregard God's commandment but cling to human tradition" (Mark 7:8). "He went on to say, "How well [meaning completely] you have set aside the commandments of God in order to uphold your tradition!" (Mark 7:9). The rabbis made up a whole new theology. It sounded like it was something from the Bible, and that was the deception. Since it sounded so good and right, how could it be wrong? But it was deadly wrong.

Though the Lord condemned it, people then and now live mostly by traditional beliefs. They bank on them, count on them, and are convinced in their minds that these traditions are the right ways to think, believe, and do things. They have been taught false doctrine all their lives and do not know the difference. False knowledge is fatal and must be corrected before it is eternally too late. The elders had the scriptures; they had the truth, but they set the Bible aside and ignored it. It is a difficult thing to leave a false belief system for something that is right when we have been taught by the religious leaders we have trusted. This may involve leaving a church family in which one has been raised. People risk suffering rejection by family and friends. They are unsure of themselves. Make no mistake, doing the right thing is hard but necessary and assures the sinner of a right relationship with God and the Lord, Jesus Christ.

If unbiblical beliefs were wrong and condemned during the Lord's earthly ministry, what makes a person think they are all right today? It is amazing that many people don't care what they believe. They never take the time to think about where they will spend eternity. Many more biblical illustrations could be given to make it clear that religious people who believed "something" are now awaiting final judgment at the throne of God. There's no escape.

Saul of Tarsus

Saul of Tarsus was a deeply religious man. He was educated in the school of Gamaliel in Jerusalem with some of Israel's finest teachers of the Mosaic law. Saul was a Pharisee and a member of the Sanhedrin Council. They were the religious leaders and rulers of Judaism. The religion of Saul's day was apostate Judaism, far from the worship system that God established for His chosen people. It was considered apostasy because it rejected Jesus of Nazareth as Israel's Messiah and Savior and because its so-called observance of the Mosaic law was hypocritical. Saul, like the rulers of the Jews, followed the traditions of the fathers—hence, "ancestral traditions"

(Galatians 1:14)—who were the false teachers of the Jews in the Old Testament. They were teachers who cast aside the Word of God and killed God's prophets.

We first hear of Saul in Acts 7:58, where he is mentioned as presiding at the stoning death of Stephen by the Sanhedrin Council. He is next mentioned in Acts 8:1–3 as the leader of the intense persecution of the Christian Church. The persecution was so severe that Christians were forced to flee for their lives out of Judea. Acts points out how dedicated this deeply religious man was when it says, "Now Saul, still breathing murderous threats against the disciples of the Lord, went to the high priest and asked for letters to the synagogues in Damascus, that, if he should find any men or women who belonged to the Way, he might bring them back to Jerusalem in chains" (Acts 9:1–2). He was extremely zealous in his efforts to eradicate Christianity, as noted in Galatians 1:14.

Saul was deeply religious, but he was not a Christian. Later, when looking back at his early life, he describes himself as a blasphemer, a persecutor, and arrogant (1 Timothy 1:13). He was physically abusive, harsh, and unforgiving. In Galatians, he says he "persecuted the church of God beyond measure and tried to destroy it" (Galatians 1:13). When he stood before King Agrippa and the governors, Festus and Felix, he testified, "I myself once thought that I had to do many things against the name of Jesus the Nazorean, and I did so in Jerusalem. I imprisoned many of the holy ones with the authorization I received from the chief priests, and when they were put to death I cast my vote against them. Many times, in synagogue after synagogue, I punished them in an attempt to force them to blaspheme; I was so enraged against them that I pursued them even to foreign cities" (Acts 26:9–12).

Why didn't God eliminate this terrible man? God had plans for Saul of Tarsus. God knows the heart of every individual, including Saul's. God had mercy on Saul because he did all those terrible things out of ignorance. He really wanted to serve God. The Lord met Saul on the road to Damascus, Assyria, a foreign city. Saul was traveling to Damascus with letters to the synagogues, giving him permission to arrest believers in Jesus and return them in chains to Jerusalem for prosecution. How totally surprised he was when he learned that Jesus of Nazareth really was Israel's Messiah. Saul, trembling and astonished, was hardly able to believe his ears. We are sure this accurately describes Saul as he lay there on the Damascus road. That very day, this deeply religious Jewish Pharisee learned how terribly wrong he had been—not only in his actions, but in his religious convictions. Nothing would do but a total change of beliefs and an abandonment of his lifestyle. So great was the change Saul experienced that even his name was changed; he was no longer called Saul of Tarsus, but rather Paul, the apostle to the whole world, both Jew and Gentile. According to Galatians 1, by special revelation, God gave Paul a brand-new gospel to preach, a gospel of salvation by grace through faith without the works of the Mosaic law. He became the greatest soul-winner, church-planter, and evangelist of all time. Paul cast aside the religion of Saul of Tarsus, the religion of apostate Judaism, and he embraced the gospel that the Lord made known to him. That is the gospel we must believe today. It has never been changed, it has not gone out of style, and it is not obsolete. It is the gospel the world needs to hear today. It is the gospel that leads lost sinners out of bondage and sin. It is not just the good news or the great news, but the greatest news: the Lord, Jesus Christ, has paid in full the wages of sin for us.

From this, we can learn the most valuable lesson—namely that religion can never save us, but Jesus Christ can and will, if we will believe what the Bible says about Him and trust in what God has done through Him to make our salvation possible, as much light of the truth as we have. The gospel still is, "Believe in the Lord Jesus and you and your household will be saved" (Acts 16:31). "For by grace you have been saved through faith, and this is not from you; it is the gift of God; it is not from works, so no one may boast" (Ephesians 2:8–9).

CHAPTER 2
TRADITION

THE DOGMAS OF many religions are based on tradition rather than on the Bible. What is tradition? It is knowledge that has been handed down by word of mouth and that has not been personally experienced. Its accuracy depends on the strength of evidence. Traditional theology is that which has been passed down verbally and, in the process of time, may be written down. The word *tradition* comes from the Greek word *paradosi,* which means "to hand over, a giving over by word of mouth or writing." This Greek word is found just thirteen times in the New Testament.

In the beginning, as far as we know, God's Word was all shared by word of mouth until Moses wrote the Pentateuch. Man walked and talked with God. Since Moses wrote every word by divine inspiration, we know what God said in the beginning. The Bible teaches that there is a good feature about tradition, and there is also a bad aspect. We need to know both. The Bible records many precepts, ethics, ordinances, customs, habits, and rituals that were passed on to us and that became traditional practices. Some were written down first, and others later, but all were recorded in scripture. There are traditions of the Lord, Jesus Christ, and the apostles that have been written down and that make up part of the writings of scripture. There are dangers in relying on unwritten traditional theology:

1. In time, long-established customs and practices take on the effect of the Bible. In fact, they replace the Bible.
2. Tradition might stand on no known facts that can be substantiated. It cannot be verified as factual.
3. When traditional teachings are passed on by word of mouth, they become subject to change by adding to them, subtracting from them, and changing them from what was originally believed into something new or different. Natural mistakes and memory failures contribute as well.
4. Tradition has the danger of being placed on equal authority with or above the Bible. Tradition is neither bad nor wrong when it is in complete, unadulterated agreement with the Bible. When tradition contradicts the Bible, however, it's tradition that's wrong—never the Bible. Wrong tradition becomes hostile to Christianity. When tradition contradicts the Bible, the Bible calls it another gospel. Through the apostle Paul, God pronounced a curse on anyone who preaches "a gospel other than the one that we preached to you" (Galatians 1:8–9). When tradition is true, it becomes a means of preserving the truth. Paul wrote in 2 Corinthians that, when one preaches another gospel, he also preaches "another Jesus," (2 Corinthians 11:4), not the Jesus who is the Son of God and the only Savior to sinners. All too often, tradition has been used as a tool of oppression and control.

Paul, the apostle to the whole world, urged his subjects to rely only on tradition that had already been recorded in scripture (2 Thessalonians 2:15). Jesus taught that some traditions were simply inventions of religious entities and were misleading, such as "the purification of cups and jugs and kettles" in Mark 7:4. Paul said to "test everything" (1 Thessalonians 5:21), meaning to put things to the test for accuracy. The people in Berea "examined the scriptures daily to determine whether these things were so" (Acts 17:11). The Lord faulted the scribes and Pharisees by saying, "In vain do they worship me, teaching as doctrines human precepts" (Mark 7:7). What was wrong with the washing of pots and cups and the washing of hands? Nothing at all. It was the spiritual significance they believed was attached to these washings that was wrong. There was no spiritual significance.

The Lord addressed the subject of authority not by saying one should ask the elders in Israel, the Sanhedrin court, or the rabbis, scribes, Pharisees, or Sadducees. He said, "Search the Scriptures" (John 5:39). The practice of inventing rules and regulations to believe and govern our lives has persisted to this day, and it is as wrong now as it was in biblical times. History shows that during the Middle Ages, (the Dark Ages, cr. AD 476 to cr. AD 1000), tradition was used to justify religious beliefs rather than the Bible. It was easy to pass on anything to the masses of uneducated and ignorant people. Those truly were the dark ages. This practice brought a storm of protest from the Reformers, who insisted that all theology had to be tested by the Bible. The Reformers had the highest regard for tradition if it followed exact, sound Bible teachings.

The Bible was the yardstick of truth. There are churches today that claim the teachings of the apostles have been handed down through the centuries by word of mouth, but, in fact, what they say the apostles taught stands in contrast to the Bible. There is not a bit of evidence that the apostles ever taught these things. Tradition often rests on the teachings of the Dark Ages and cannot be traced further back in history. There is no proof whatsoever that those doctrines were ever taught or believed by the early church or first-century Christians.

If *tradition* means "passed on by word of mouth," then that is how the truth about the grace of God is being spread around the world today. Some cultures do not have Bibles or even a written language, but they do have biblical teachers. The gospel is spread abroad by word of mouth, and that is good. By word of mouth is what Paul taught Timothy: "And what you [Timothy] heard from me [Paul] through many witnesses entrust to faithful people who will have the ability to teach others as well" (2 Timothy 2:2). But never is the gospel in contrast to the scriptures. The gospel was the scriptures. In the end, we must obey God rather than men.

If we are taught the traditions of the church but the church has erred, is there a way to discover these errors and correct them? Some errors are easy to detect. If a child has been told that two apples and two more apples equal five apples, will he be able to see the error? In school, he or she will be taught numbers and arithmetic. That which is right can be seen. It's no problem at all to figure that two plus two do not equal five. A child can see with his or her eyes, count on his or her fingers, conclude correctly that two plus two equals four, and can prove it with an easy observable experiment. The child's conclusion would be correct and reasonable. When we are taught a dogma that is not true or correct, it helps to have something to appeal to—something observable—and that something is the Bible. The Bible uncovers errors; it exposes them. Set what we are taught alongside what the Bible teaches, and if they are not the same or alike, we need to find out why. Find the problem and make the correction. God's Word is always right.

Many church traditions were established at the Council of Trent (1545–1563). The council was organized to counter the Reformation (1517–1648). The council's purpose was to expose, condemn, and refute Protestant beliefs like those set forth by Martin Luther, John Calvin, and others. In doing so, the council made clear the beliefs of the Roman Catholic Church. The first meetings were attended by about forty men, most of whom were Catholic bishops. They met about twenty-five times over a period of eighteen years. The Reformers believed that a sinner was justified by faith alone, apart from good works or keeping the Mosaic law. The council declared that the Reformers' teachings were heresy, and those who believed them were anathema. *Anathema* means that the church pronounced a curse on the believer who was then excommunicated and condemned to eternal judgment.

The Reformers rejected the Apocrypha as part of the canon of scripture. The council issued a decree, damning anyone who rejected the Apocrypha. Let him or her be anathema, they declared. Teachings like Purgatory, prayers for the dead, and salvation by works are taught in the Apocrypha.

Nearly all the Reformers rejected the doctrine of transubstantiation—namely, the changing of the communion wine into the literal blood of Christ and the wafer into the literal body of Christ. The Council of Trent said of those who rejected this doctrine, let them be anathema.

Although the Reformers said the only source of doctrinal truth was the Bible, the council said there were two sources of truth: the Bible and tradition. Those who rejected the testimony of tradition were anathema. The Reformers rejected indulgences as a means of pardon from temporal punishment. The Church did not promote the selling of indulgences, but neither did they take steps to ban the practice. It made money. The Reformers rejected the doctrine of purgatory, a place of temporal punishment for venial sins. The council affirmed the teaching of purgatory and condemned all who rejected it. The Reformers were anathema.

The Reformers also rejected the practice of celibacy for priests. The Church said that marriage was valid only if the ceremony was performed by a priest and witnessed by two individuals. They condemned divorce. The Reformers rejected the changing of the Julian calendar. Pope Gregory XIII requested that the council make such a change and make it known as the Gregorian calendar, by which it is still known today.

There are many other doctrines, practices, and beliefs that the council promoted and on which they pronounced anathemas to all who rejected them. The Second Vatican Council, held from 1962 to 1965, confirmed all that the Council of Trent declared. Nothing was changed. What was adjudged as the teachings of the Church make up the catechisms of today, so that, today, we read in the *C. I. S. Extension Course*, revised edition of the *Baltimore Catechism*, number 3, part 1, chapter 2, page 23: "Tradition is the unwritten word of God – the body of truths revealed by God to the Apostles, and not committed by them to writing but handed down by word of mouth."

Synonyms are words that have similar meanings. For example, *afflict, torment, oppress, bother,* and *distress* all mean the same thing with only slight shades of difference between them. The word *tradition* has no synonyms in the New Testament. *Paradosis* is always translated as *tradition* in its thirteen occurrences, except in 1 Corinthians 11:2, where it is translated as *ordinances.*

Tradition is used to signify transmission of ideas without saying where they came from, how the information was transmitted, or what time had elapsed. The weakness of traditional teachings and their contrast with biblical doctrines demands that the validity of tradition be challenged. Tradition is based wholly on assumptions. Assumed theology should always be open and subject to criticism and examination, no matter who says it. Every doctrine ought to be put to the test—and the test is, is it scriptural? Does it say what the Bible says, or does it contradict the Bible? If it cannot be found in the Bible, it should never be considered God's word.

Paul, apostle to the world, once followed the traditional teachings of the elders in Israel. He learned his theology from his family, the school of Gamaliel, the elders, Pharisees, and the rabbis. He was zealous in upholding the traditions of the fathers, but when he was converted on the Damascus road, he abandoned these when the Lord showed him that what he believed was wrong. He changed his beliefs from the traditions of his fathers to the doctrinal truths that the Lord revealed to him. He changed from humankind's traditions to God's revealed Word. He abandoned apostate Judaism and the rabbinical doctrines in which he had been raised. We need to take a lesson from Paul. Everyone in doctrinal error needs to be corrected and follow Paul.

Tradition has been used as a tool of repression, a control

mechanism. People have been told not to bother reading the Bible. "We'll tell you what to believe," they are told. Suggesting that the Bible is the mind of God and that it is too difficult for ordinary people to understand is another admonition. That's the lie the devil wants people to believe. Tradition opens the door for teaching everything and anything that can never be verified one way or another. Rome exalts the church and its hierarchy. Christianity exalts the Lord, Jesus Christ, and the Word of God. If it is taught that the church cannot err, then that teaching must be challenged. We know that tradition is wrong when it contradicts the Bible. We know that traditional doctrines are subject to serious doubt when they are not mentioned in the Bible.

There seems to be a link between philosophy and tradition. Philosophy is what people think about this and that, but there is an emptiness to it all. We need to know what God thinks about this and that. Paul taught orally, but he taught only God's Word. Paul's teachings became the traditions of the early church. They still govern the lives of believers today. Paul wrote them down. That makes them unchangeable. Does it matter if what we believe are unverified traditions?

CHAPTER 3

MARY

DOES ANYONE WORSHIP Mary, the mother of Jesus? Protestants do not believe it is right to worship Mary. Catholics also say they do not worship Mary; rather, they honor her as the mother of Jesus. In Luke 1:26–35 and 1:48, we read that an angel appeared to Mary with the greeting, "Hail, favored one! the Lord is with you" (Luke 1:28). Mary says, "behold, from now on will all ages call me blessed" (Luke 1:48). From this passage in the gospel of Luke, the Catholic Church has assumed that Mary was chosen because of who she was and was especially blessed above all other women in Israel. But this passage does not say such things. In Luke 1:42, it plainly says that she was blessed among women, not above women. The generations mentioned in verse forty-eight are those of the people of Israel, not all the people in the world throughout all ages. It is no secret that the Jews knew their Messiah would be a Jew and that many women in Israel hoped they could be the mother of the Messiah. The Greek text does not say Mary was highly favored because of who or what she was—namely, a woman supposedly born without sin. The scriptures contradict the teaching that Mary was sinless. The veneration given to Mary by the Catholic Church looks very much like worship to outsiders. It has been noted that much more is said about her than about Jesus Christ in Catholic writings, newspapers, books, magazines, and other literature.

To know about Mary and her place in God's plan, we will consult the Bible only—specifically, the *New American Bible* (NABRE), published by the World Catholic Press, a division of Catholic Book Publishing, using the 2011 edition. Does the NABRE teach that Mary was the mother of God or that she was born without sin? Does it teach that she remained a virgin after Jesus was born or that she ascended bodily into heaven after being resurrected? Where does the NABRE say that Mary can now hear our prayers, that she has the power to heal anyone, or that she ever performed one miracle? Where is there a passage that says everyone must go through her to approach Jesus Christ? Where are we commanded to pray to her? Where does it say that she is a mediator? Is there a passage that says she is or should be honored with images of her? Does the Catholic Bible say anywhere that she can save a soul or even help save a soul from damnation and judgment in the lake of fire? Is there a verse in the NABRE that says she is the mother of the Church or has issued commands that we are to obey? This is a partial list of doctrines that are highly suspect and that we intend to challenge. The above gives us plenty to study and weigh honestly and carefully.

Who Was Mary?

Mary was a young Jewish girl living in Nazareth of Galilee around 4 BC (Luke 1:26). In Hebrew, her name was Miriam. Her father was Heli, a descendant of King David, thus placing her in the royal family of Israel, the tribe of Judah (Luke 3:24). Heli became the father-in-law of Joseph, Mary's husband-to-be. She had a cousin named Elizabeth who, with her husband, was of the priestly family of Israel, the tribe of Levi. Mary was espoused to a Jewish man named Joseph, who was also of the royal family of Israel (Luke 1:27). This means that if Israel still had Jewish kings reigning over them, Joseph would have been their king—the only man in Israel with that right. But there was no Jewish king when Jesus was born because God had taken the kingdom away from Israel, and their line of kings had no place to rule. They lost their kingdom because of sin, especially the sin of idolatry. It was Joseph and Mary who were going to be the parents of the next king of Israel when the nation's kingdom was restored to them. Instead of being Israel's king, Joseph was a carpenter in Nazareth. The Bible says he was a righteous man (Matthew 1:19). No other kind of man would have served as the adopted father of Jesus.

Before the marriage ceremony between Joseph and Mary took place, Mary "was found with child" (Matthew 1:18). How could Mary explain this to Joseph? It is hard to imagine what went through her mind as she broke the news to him. She probably rehearsed several ways of revealing this to Joseph. And how did Joseph take the news? He didn't believe her. Who would? From the beginning of creation, a child conceived always had a human father and human mother. What happened with Mary had never happened before in history. Joseph may have loved Mary, but due to her disclosure, he decided against marrying her. Instead, he tried to find a way to divorce her, and protect her from the judgment ordered by the Mosaic Law at the same time. The law stated that Mary should have been put to death by stoning (Leviticus 20:10; Deuteronomy 22:20–23). Alternately, Mary could have been burned (Genesis 38:24; Leviticus 21:9).

Joseph wanted to divorce her quietly, as noted in Matthew 1:19. "Such was his intention" (Matthew 1:20), but this hardly explains the depth of his problem. While he thought on these things, he wrestled with the problem of how to divorce Mary quietly. After all, the public would most likely implicate him as the father, and the law could insist that he marry her, which would have saved her from being stoned or burned. The son to be born would have been tainted and considered born out of wedlock, subject to a life of unearned abuse. It is certain that Joseph spent some very restless nights lying awake, thinking about, planning, and going over and over the issues involved. What would their parents think? What would the public think? Joseph was unable to resolve these problems, but he didn't need a plan. God already had the problems solved and revealed this to Joseph. God sent His angel, who confirmed what Mary had told Joseph. It was true; she was with child by the supernatural work of the Holy Spirit of God, who caused her to be pregnant. Joseph was ordered by God to "not be afraid to take Mary your wife into your home" (Matthew 1:20). Joseph did so without delay in obedience to the Lord.

Mary was one of seven women in the Bible who bore that name in the New Testament. Mary, the mother of Jesus, is mentioned nineteen times by name in the four gospels and once in Acts 1:14, but after that, she is never mentioned by name again in the New Testament. She is also mentioned by the following pronouns: *her* eighteen times; *she* six times; *you* and *your* fourteen times; *I* three times; *me* and *my* six times; *mother* twenty-eight times; and *wife* two times. In addition, there are other references to Mary, such as *virgin* three times; *woman*, one time; *handmaid* two times; *betrothed* one time; and *servant* one time. So, by name and all other references, that's a total of 104 references. In comparison, Peter is mentioned by name alone 164 times. Saul of Tarsus and Paul are mentioned by name 186 times.

If we were to include pronouns and other references to them, the number for these two men would be much greater. There is no mention of Mary's birth or death. She is never mentioned in Old Testament prophecy, unless Genesis 3:15 and Isaiah 7:14 refer to her. It is of special interest that Simon Peter, said to be the first bishop and first in the line of popes in Rome, wrote two New Testament epistles and never mentioned her once. John, the disciple, wrote five New Testament books and mentioned her only once, in John 2:1–5, but not by name. That's all the stranger when we check the record and see that when Jesus was crucified, He entrusted his mother into the care of John the disciple (John 19:26–27).

James and Jude each wrote one New Testament epistle and were most assuredly her sons, but they never mention her once. All this is very strange in view of the attention given to her today by the Roman Catholic Church. Furthermore, the Lord, Jesus, did not give Mary special recognition, neither did He ever indicate that she was to be remembered in future ages. Yet, many doctrines have been taught about her person and work that, when compared with the Bible, raise serious questions.

The Perpetual Virginity of Mary

Nowhere in the Bible do we find the teaching of the perpetual virginity of Mary. This doctrine asserts that after Jesus was born, she remained a virgin. In fact, the Bible clearly contradicts this. First, Jesus's younger brothers and sisters are mentioned in the following passages: Matthew 12:46–50 and 13:55; Mark 3:31–34; Luke 8:19–21; John 2:12, 7:3–5, and 7:10; and Acts 1:14. A summary of these passages reveals that there was a close association between Mary and the four brothers and sisters. If they were Mary's children, why wouldn't there be? According to John 7:3–5, his brothers did not believe that Jesus was the prophesied Messiah of Israel; therefore, they could not have been His disciples or apostles at that time. The Catholic Church says they were cousins of Jesus. There is a word in the Greek text for relatives who are cousins—see Luke 1:36 and 1:58, and Colossians 4:10.

If cousins were what the inspired scriptures meant, why not use that word instead of *brothers*? The family lived in Nazareth of Galilee. Why are the unbelieving cousins traveling around Galilee and Judea with their aunt, if that's what she was to them? And why does there seem to be a family association between Joseph and the children in the verses mentioned above? It seems reasonable to conclude that these four men were literally the younger half-siblings of Jesus and were the sons of Mary and Joseph. The public thought they were. Didn't people know the difference between a cousin and a son? Why should we think differently than the public? We also read in Luke that when Jesus was born, Mary "gave birth to her firstborn son" (Luke 2:7). In checking various dictionaries, we find them to be in perfect agreement that the word *firstborn* means "first in a family." Jesus was the firstborn or, in other words, the oldest child of Joseph and Mary, strongly implying that there were other children born to Mary after Jesus. When we read their names in Matthew 13:55, why should we not believe that the men mentioned were the younger brothers? Mary had at least seven children, five sons and two or more daughters. How could she have remained a virgin? Jesus was the firstborn of Mary, but He was the only Son of God (John 3:16). Joseph accepted and treated Jesus as his son. Does it matter what we believe about who Jesus was and His ancestry? It mattered enough to God to make an accurate historical record of it. Mary did not remain a virgin after Jesus was born.

The Immaculate Conception

The Immaculate Conception does not refer to Mary conceiving Jesus, but rather, to Mary being conceived by her mother. Was Mary born without sin? Is her supposed sinless condition a scriptural doctrine? What we know about sinners is that God inspired Paul to write "all have sinned" (Romans 3:23) about the human race. The lone exception is Jesus Himself; He never sinned. The following scriptures in the NABRE say clearly and plainly that Jesus never sinned: 2 Corinthians 5:21 explains that He "did not know sin"; 1 Peter 1:19 says He was "a spotless unblemished lamb"; and 1 John 3:5 tells us that "in him is no sin." No wonder the Jews could not accuse the Lord of sin in John 8:46 when He challenged them to prove that He had sinned. No such statement is found in the Bible about Mary.

All who sin need a savior who can forgive them and save them from sin's penalty. Did Mary need a Savior? Note her words in the Magnificat in Luke, where she says, "my spirit rejoices in God my savior" (Luke 1:47). Mary knew that she was not without sin, that she needed a Savior, and that perhaps the child to whom she would give birth would be her Savior. Jesus said to the rich young ruler, "Why do you ask me about the good? There is only One who is good" (Matthew 19:17).

Jesus was Emmanuel, God in the flesh. Mary was good, but she was not without sin. The apostle Paul says, "He [Christ] is the head of the body, the church. He is the beginning, the firstborn from the dead, that in all things he himself might be preeminent" (Colossians 1:18). Jesus Christ alone is the preeminent one, but reading through Catholic literature, one does not get that impression. Mary is highly preeminent—too preeminent, not only in their literature, but also in their forms of worship. What difference is there between honor and worship? What the Church insists is honor is, in actuality, worship. "A rose by any other name smells the same," Shakespeare says.

The Mother of God

Is Mary the mother of God? The reasoning is that, if Jesus was God, and Mary gave birth to Jesus, then she would also be the mother of God. This is faulty reasoning. All fundamental Christians believe in Mary, but they do not believe more than what the Bible ascribes to her. They believe that:

1. Mary was blessed by God to be the earthly mother of Jesus.
2. Mary was holy, pure, and good.
3. Mary conceived Jesus by the Holy Spirit of God.
4. Mary was a virgin when Jesus was born but not after.

What fundamental Christians do not believe is that:

1. Mary was ever prayed to by anyone in the Bible or that she can now hear or answer a prayer today.
2. Mary was the chief of all saints.
3. When she was conceived by her mother, she was born without sin.

4. She never sinned.
5. She was resurrected after she died and went, bodily, directly to heaven.
6. She had a part in humankind's redemption or could ever be coredemptrix with Christ.
7. She was ever in Rome.
8. She performed a miracle while here on earth or after she supposedly went to heaven.
9. She is the gate to heaven or the queen of heaven.
10. She was the mother of God.
11. Mary was blessed above other women to be the mother of Jesus (Luke 1:42).

Why do fundamental Christians deny all these doctrines and many more about Mary? The simple answer is because not one of these beliefs can be found in the Bible. They are all based on tradition; they are unscriptural and contradict the Bible. Not one of them can be verified.

Mary's Virgin Birth of Jesus

There are three main positions held about the virgin birth of Jesus:

1. It never happened because it is humanly and naturally impossible for a child to be born without an earthly father;
2. The virgin birth happened, but more is attributed to it than can be attested to by scriptures; or
3. The virgin birth is a fact of history, but nothing more and nothing less is believed about it than what the Bible says.

It seems biblically correct to accept the third position as right because it has the least amount of objection and the most scripture to support it. How is it possible to hold an adequate view of the virgin birth of Jesus if it is denied or embellished beyond the provable facts stated in the Bible? We have in the Bible God's trustworthy account for it. What is taught about the virgin birth by tradition is untrustworthy because it is impossible to verify it. All one has is somebody's word for it, and that is not enough, no matter whose word it is. If what one believes about Mary is in the Bible, that makes it a fact that can be attested to.

If the virgin birth is denied when the Bible says it is a fact of history, this then leads to a greater problem—namely, the integrity of the scriptures. Can the Bible be trusted as the inspired word of God if it errs? How can the Bible be trusted in whole if it cannot be trusted in part and vice versa? If parts of the Bible cannot be trusted as factual truth, who is qualified to decide which parts are trustworthy, which are not, and on what basis?

To add more details to the Bible than what is already written leads to no end of unrestrained ideas. Some have thought that, in order to be the Lord's mother, Mary had to be born without sin and that God gave her a special, pure soul. This concept is called the Immaculate Conception. It is further taught that Mary was resurrected after she died and was taken directly to heaven; this is called the Assumption. It is further taught that after Jesus was born, Mary remained a virgin. All these doctrines are based on tradition.

If Jesus was God, then why isn't Mary the mother of God? Jesus is the eternal Son of God, meaning, He lived in eternity past and has always been a member of the triune Godhead. As a member of the Godhead of Father, Son, and Holy Spirit, Jesus was God and remained so even after He was born into this world. In Isaiah, we read, "Therefore the Lord himself will give you a sign; the young woman, pregnant and about to bear a son, shall name Him Emmanuel" (Isaiah 7:14). Matthew quotes Isaiah 7:14 and gives the interpretation of His name, *Emmanuel*, which means "God is with us" (Matthew 1:23). Compare this with the statements in Luke: "And the angel said unto her in reply, 'the holy Spirit will come upon you, and the power of the Most High will overshadow you. Therefore the child to be born will be called holy, the Son of God'"

(Luke 1:35). "When Elizabeth heard Mary's greeting, the infant [John the Baptist] leaped in her womb, and Elizabeth, filled with the Holy Spirit, cried out in a loud voice and said, "Most blessed are you among women, and blessed is the fruit of your womb. And how does this happen to me, that the mother of my Lord should come to me?" (Luke 1:41–43). In view of these statements, is it correct to refer to Mary as the mother of God? Can fundamental Christians be justified in denying that she was the mother of God?

First, *God* is a noun in English and grammatically is a singular noun. That is not the case in Greek or Hebrew, where *God* is a plural noun. He is one God with three distinct personalities: Father, Son, and Holy Spirit. In the Old Testament, Genesis begins, "In the beginning when God created" (Genesis 1:1). The Hebrew word for *God* is plural. This is why, in Genesis, plural pronouns are used in reference to God: "let us" and "after our likeness" (Genesis 1:26). Who was God talking to? All three personalities of the Godhead were involved in the creation process. Was Mary the mother of the Father or of the Holy Spirit?

If Mary was the mother of Jesus, how can anyone deny that she was the mother of God? Jesus, the Son of God, was there in the beginning when creation was taking place, and He is the person of the Godhead who did the creating. God, the Father, issued the decree to create everything, and God, the Son, in obedience to the Father, did the actual work of creating. This is what the Bible says. Paul says that Christ, though not mentioned by name, is preeminent and supreme as God's agent in the creation of all things (Colossians 1:15–18). John's gospel says, "All things came to be through him, and without him nothing came to be" (John 1:3). These statements are further supported in the NABRE by Ephesians 3:9, 1 Corinthians 8:6, and Revelation 4:11. Jesus Christ is the eternal Son of God, who never had a beginning. To be the Son of God was understood to be God. That's what the Jews correctly understood. John says, "For this reason the Jews tried all the more to kill him, because he not only broke the sabbath but he also called God his own father, making himself equal to God" (John 5:18). Mary was chosen to be the mother of Jesus but without her being the originator of His personality. It is correct to call Mary the mother of Jesus, but we must do so with the understanding that His birth did not mark the beginning of His existence. She is never called the mother of God, who is a triune being in the Bible. In fact, there are not many references to her at all. Amazing! Her name is found in the first three gospels, but never in John. The apostle Paul, who wrote at least thirteen epistles in the New Testament and founded numerous churches, never mentions her name. Neither do James and Jude.

Mary did not make one contribution to Jesus's physical existence at all. Jesus's body was created by the Father, according to Hebrews, which says, "For this reason, when he came into the world, he said, "Sacrifice and offering you did not desire, but a body you prepared for me'" (Hebrews 10:5). A reference note in the NABRE says that this refers to the incarnation, and with this, there is general agreement. Mary did not contribute a molecule, a drop of blood, a gene, a personality trait, or anything else to the body or person of the Lord, Jesus Christ.

Mary was truly a godly woman and should be respected as such. She was probably a young girl, perhaps in her teens, but was not part of the aristocracy of Israel, as if that would matter to God. She was well versed in the scriptures and could quote them. She acknowledged God's mercy, holiness, and strength. There is no reason from scripture to refer to her today as the Blessed Virgin or the Virgin Mary. She is so-called because of the mistaken belief that she remained a virgin after Jesus was born. The Bible presents an entirely different picture. Matthew says that Joseph "had no relations with her until she bore a son, and he named him Jesus" (Matthew 1:25). Having no marital relationship with Mary assured that he could not have been the father. The word *until* implies that, after Jesus was born, the relationship between Joseph and Mary changed into a normal married relationship.

When Jesus grew to manhood and began His ministry, the

Jews were astonished at His preaching. It was far different than the preaching of the rabbis, scribes, and Pharisees. They wondered how the son of a carpenter, who was not educated, could preach what He did. They said, "Is he not the carpenter's son? Is not his mother named Mary and his brothers James, Joseph, Simon, and Judas? Are not his sisters all with us?" (Matthew 13:55–56). They were all part of a single family. Greek grammar and vocabulary will not allow for any other rendering.

Fundamental Christians have as much respect for Mary as Jesus did, and as much as the twelve disciples and others around showed her. There is nothing in the scriptural record to indicate that she influenced Jesus during His earthly ministry, though there were times when she might have attempted to do so. She never interceded spiritually for anyone and was never in any way part of God's plan of redemption. She was never—then or now—a mediator between humankind and God, and she was never the hope of sinners.

The only mediator mentioned in the Bible is the Lord, Jesus Christ. Paul wrote, "For there is one God. There is also one mediator between God and the human race, Christ Jesus, himself human" (1 Timothy 2:5). A mediator is one who intercedes for others, one who brings about a peaceable relationship. Take, for example, the statement in Hebrews, "Therefore, he is always able to save those who approach God through him [Jesus Christ] since he lives forever to make intercession for them" (Hebrews 7:25). There is no Mary in those words. In the epistle to the Romans, it says, "Therefore, since we have been justified by faith, we have peace with God through our Lord Jesus Christ" (Romans 5:1). Not through Mary.

Again, in Ephesians, we read, "For he [Christ] is our peace," (Ephesians 2:14); that is to say, our source of peace with God. Many other Bible verses say basically the same things—too many to list here. The Lord, Jesus Christ, alone is our source of peace with God because He mediates for us. Mary is never once mentioned as serving in that capacity. She is not the only hope of sinners. She offers no hope at all.

All our hope rests in the Lord, Jesus Christ, which is why Paul says to his coworker Timothy, "Paul, an apostle of Christ Jesus by command of God our savior and of Christ Jesus our hope" (1 Timothy 1:1). Jesus Christ is our everything. He is all we need. He is the light of the world, the way, the truth, and the life. He is the only Savior to lost sinners. Not one of these things is said about Mary in the Bible. She needed God to save her the same as all others of Adam's race. It was a great privilege for Mary to be the mother of Jesus, but in the end, it cost her a great price when she saw her innocent firstborn son cruelly crucified as a lawbreaking criminal. A careful search of the scriptures will separate fact from fiction. It matters altogether what we believe about Mary.

CHAPTER 4

SIMON PETER

SIMON PETER WAS one of the Lord's twelve apostles and was named by the Lord in Matthew 10:2 as the *protos*. *Protos*, a Greek word, means "chief, leader, or head," and indeed, he was the chief spokesman for the twelve as the scriptures bear out. Was he also the bishop in Rome and the first in the long line of popes? In fact, was he ever in Rome at all? These and other scriptural details about this disciple and apostle are the subjects of this chapter.

In the closing chapter of Paul's epistle to the Roman Christians, Paul mentions no less than twenty-five church members by name, plus others who are not named. The epistle was written about two years before Paul's arrival in Rome. There must be a reason why he did not mention Simon Peter. If Peter had been in Rome and was the bishop of the church, then surely Paul would have been remiss in not acknowledging him. The omission of Peter's name raises some serious questions.

If Peter was in Rome serving as the first bishop of the church, then why would Paul have thought it necessary to visit there? We do not have to guess about the answer because Paul gives the reason in Romans 1:7–15. Paul says he wants to visit the church in Rome, "that I may share with you some spiritual gift so that you may be strengthened" (Romans 1:11). Paul says he wants to visit them to "harvest some fruit among you, too, as among the rest of the Gentiles" (Romans 1:13). He adds, "I am under obligation; that is why I am eager to preach the gospel also to you in Rome" (Romans 1:14–15). There are some strong implications in these verses. One implication is that nobody was sufficiently preaching the gospel and teaching the Christians in Rome, thus making Paul's ministry a necessity. What work was the first bishop doing if he was there?

Paul wrote thirteen epistles—fourteen, if he wrote Hebrews—and he never once recognized Peter as the bishop or pope over all the churches. That constitutes a colossal omission. Paul said he preached the gospel where others had not preached. "Thus I aspire to proclaim the gospel not where Christ has already been named, so that I do not build on another's foundation" (Romans 15:20). To the Corinthians, Paul makes a similar statement: "So that we may preach the gospel even beyond you, not boasting of work already done in another's sphere" (2 Corinthians 10:16). If Peter was in Rome at any time, it would have been against Paul's policy to go there, building on another man's foundation and repeating work that had already been done.

The Lord named Simon Peter the *protos*. This Greek word, which translates as the "first" in Greek, is used often in the Greek New Testament (157 times) to designate the role of leadership or importance. The Lord gave to Peter the "keys to the kingdom" (Matthew 16:19), but the Lord never proclaimed Peter as the bishop of the Roman church or the pope of all the Christian churches. Peter's work was strictly limited to Israel and the Jews. As the scriptural record shows, he is never mentioned leaving Israel except when he went to Antioch of Syria, where Paul confronted him for duplicity (Galatians 2:11–14). Paul admonished Peter publicly for trying to bring Gentiles under the yoke of the Mosaic law and Judaism.

When was the last time a ranking dignitary of the church confronted the pope publicly for bad behavior, false teaching, and bad leadership? Peter was a disciple, an apostle, a preacher, a member, and a chief leader of the church in Jerusalem, but he was most assuredly never in Rome, was not the first bishop in Rome, or the first pope. The Bible supports the view that he was the apostle to Israel.

During the Lord's earthy ministry, Peter believed that Jesus was the Christ, Israel's Messiah. According to Matthew 16:21–23, he did not believe that Jesus would die for his sins or the sins of the world. Peter believed that the Messiah would restore Israel's lost kingdom and reign as king of the Jews and liberate Israel from Roman rule. His view did not change until after the Lord's crucifixion, burial, resurrection, and ascension. When Jesus was crucified, Peter didn't even believe the Lord would be raised from the dead. He became a believer in the risen Lord only when he saw Him in His risen state.

If Peter was to become the bishop in Rome and the first pope, why didn't the Lord make this known? Why didn't James, Jude, and John, who combined to write seven New Testament books, make this known? Why didn't Peter, who wrote two New Testament books, reinforce his bishopric in his writings? Matthew 16 presents an especially difficult problem concerning Peter. Few verses in the Bible have more views set forth by some very competent scholars. The verse reads, "And so I say to you, you are Peter, and upon this rock I will build my church, and the gates of the netherworld shall not prevail against it" (Matthew 16:18).

First, this verse is prophetic. We know this because the verbs are in the future tense; hence, the statement looks forward to a future event. Second, in the Greek text, the gender for the words *Peter* and *rock* are different. *Peter* is masculine, and *rock* is feminine, so it hardly seems likely that Peter could be the rock. The rule of Greek grammar is that they must agree in gender. These words are both nouns but have different cases. *Peter* is set in the nominative case, and *rock* is in the dative case. *Church* is also a feminine-gendered noun, so this seems to imply in some way that the rock is the church. Peter is *petros* in Greek, which is the word for a stone small enough to be held in the hand. *Rock* is *petra*, meaning a "large rock or boulder or a ledge"—certainly nothing that could be held in the hand. Rocks used for the foundation of a building were *petra* rocks. *Petros* stones were never foundation stones. Peter was a small stone, not a foundational rock.

Third, who or what did the rock represent? The Lord asked His disciples who they thought He was. Peter answered, "You are the Messiah, the Son of the living God" (Matthew 16:16). Some believe that Peter was the rock. Other scholars believe that it was Peter's confession that was the rock on which Christ would build His church. Still, others say that it was not the statement itself, but rather the person of the Lord, Jesus Christ, who is the rock. When the testimony of the Old Testament is taken into consideration, it sounds like Christ is the rock.

1. Deuteronomy 32:3–4 says, "For I will proclaim the name of the Lord, praise the greatness of our God! The Rock—how faultless are his deeds,…just and upright is he." The Rock is a person. Verses fifteen, eighteen, and thirty-one also refer to the rock.
2. 1 Samuel 2:2 says, "There is no Holy One like the Lord; there is no Rock like our God."
3. 2 Samuel 22:47 says, "The Lord lives! Blessed be my rock! Exalted be God, the rock of my salvation."
4. Psalm 18:2–3 says, "He said; I love you, Lord, my strength, Lord, my rock, my fortress, my deliverer."
5. 1 Corinthians 10:4 says, "and all drank the same spiritual drink, for they drank from a spiritual rock that followed them, and the rock was the Christ."
6. 1 Peter 2:6–8 says, "For it says in scripture: "Behold, I am laying a stone in Zion, a cornerstone, chosen, and precious, and whoever believes in it shall not be put to shame." Therefore, its value is for you who have faith, but for those without faith: "The stone which the builders rejected has

become the cornerstone," and "a stone that will make people stumble, and a rock that will make them fall." Peter refers to Christ, not himself.

The verses above give reason to believe that the rock the Lord referred to in Matthew 16:18 was Himself, the Messiah, the Son of the living God. We conclude,

1. The rock is a person.
2. The point by metonymy is to illustrate the steadfastness and greatness of God.
3. The rock, Christ, will be the foundation upon which Christ will build His church.
4. The church will be Jewish, composed of the remnant of Jews who have believed in and obeyed God.
5. The Jewish remnant will be those who come out of the seven years of the Tribulation and enter into the millennial kingdom that Christ will restore to Israel after His Second Coming.
6. The rock is Christ, not Simon Peter. The millennial kingdom church is not the Roman Catholic Church.

The church that is built on Christ and not on people can never be overpowered by the authorities of Hades. Christ was rejected by the Jews, but in time, He will triumph over all rejection. He is not the head of the corner or the cornerstone yet, but He will become so at the Second Coming. Not all Jews will be part of the millennial church, only those who will be the remnant out of "the sand of the sea" (Romans 9:25–27). The Jews will be a light to the Gentiles and will win many of them to Christ. The remnant will be the living stones mentioned in 1 Peter 2:5, who make up the millennial church.

The church mentioned in Matthew 16:18 is not the church that Paul calls the body of Christ. The body of Christ is being formed today and is neither Jew nor Gentile. This church was a mystery hidden in the mind of God and unknown until God revealed it to the apostle Paul. The Lord's twelve disciples and the Old Testament prophets did not know about the body of Christ; it was a mystery to them.

Peter was the chief of the twelve, but this did not make him the dictator over them. He was the chief speaker for them, but this did not prevent the other disciples from speaking. Peter was a servant and not a lord. To press an interpretation on Matthew 16:18 that is unnatural and errant is heresy. There are those who have erred in making Peter the rock and knew they were in error, but they did not have the courage to step forth and admit it. They are afraid to acknowledge their error because it could lead to excommunication from the church. Fear keeps them locked in error and keeps them from attempting to escape from it.

What a wonderful rock the Lord is. He is the rock who never errs and never lies, who never sins, and who never needs forgiveness. He is the rock who never needed to be taught before He could teach others. He already knew it all, and He is the only know-it-all in the universe. Peter was the chief but not a prince in Israel; a senior but not a superior; a pillar in the church in Jerusalem, but not the only pillar. In Galatians 2:9, we note that James and John were also pillars in the church, and it can be supposed that the same is true of the rest of the twelve disciples.

Peter's Denial

Some historical accounts in the Bible are recorded in all four gospels of Matthew, Mark, Luke, and John. Other accounts are found in just three gospels, commonly called the Synoptic Gospels (Matthew, Mark, and Luke). Some accounts occur in just two gospels, and a few are found in only one gospel. The account of Peter's denial of personally knowing the Lord and being one of Jesus's followers is found in all four gospels (see Matthew 26:69–75, Mark 14:66–72, Luke 22:54–62, and John 18:15–27). When we line up the accounts side by side, we get a complete picture of what happened in Jerusalem when Christ was arrested and tried in Pilate's court. There are no contradictions; there is perfect agreement. Each account complements the others. When one account has details not mentioned in the others, the information is supplementary.

Peter is harshly judged for denying that he personally knew the Lord, Jesus Christ, or that he was ever one of His disciples. Yet, who among us have been bold enough to admit to those around us that we are Christians who love the Lord? We are timid, reluctant, and fear the rejection directed toward those who believe in Christ. But we are quick to judge others. Peter was fearful, as were all the disciples, and hid in moments of weakness.

Peter's denial did not catch the Lord by surprise. He predicted it. Mark records, "Then Jesus said to him [Peter], "Amen, I say to you, this very night before the cock crows twice you will deny me three times" (Mark 14:30). In Palestine, and perhaps everywhere else, a rooster crows two times. The first time is in the darkness around midnight. The second time is in the early morning as the day is beginning to dawn. The Lord had made it clear that before the rooster crowed at the dawning of day, Peter would already have denied three times that he knew the Lord or that he was His disciple.

When the Lord was arrested in the garden of Gethsemane, scripture says that the disciples fled (Matthew 26:56). The Lord asked the temple guards, who bound Him and led Him out of the garden, not to arrest the disciples (John 18:8). Most of the disciples fled and went into hiding for fear of being arrested also, but apparently, John followed the crowd to the palace of Caiaphas, the high priest. Peter also followed from afar, it says, and stayed hidden by the darkness so as not to be seen. When the large multitude arrived at the palace, John went inside with them, but Peter remained outside until John came and asked the guard to let Peter in.

Peter went into the courtyard. Because it was a cold night, a fire had been kindled, and he joined those trying to stay warm. It is amazing that there was so much activity in those wee hours of the morning. The secret arrest of Jesus had caused quite a stir. A girl who was a maid of the high priest studied Peter and concluded that he was one of the Lord's followers. She brought the matter up before those gathered around the fire, saying, "You too were with the Nazarene, Jesus" (Mark 14:67). In effect, Peter's reply was, "I don't know what you're talking about" (Mark 14:68). A while later, another maid saw Peter and announced to those present, "This man is one of them" (Mark 14:69), meaning that Peter was one of the Lord's disciples. Again, Peter denied being a disciple of Jesus. A short time later, the people standing about in the courtyard began to assert that Peter was indeed Jesus's disciple. "Surely you are one of them; for you too are a Galilean" (Mark 14:70).

At this point, Peter began to curse and swear, saying, "I do not know this man about whom you are talking" Mark 14:71. We think of cursing as profanity, but that is not what the biblical word *curse* means. It means that Peter was calling for a curse to be placed upon him if he was not telling the truth. But he was not telling the truth, and he can be grateful that no curse ever befell him. We find similar instances in scripture, where people bound themselves with a curse for one reason or another. In Acts 23:12–14, a band of Jews who hated Paul, bound themselves with a curse that they would neither eat nor drink until they had killed Paul. Since they were unable to kill Paul, we wonder how many of them died of thirst or starvation. How about, none of them? It seems that those curses didn't have much impact on people.

Mark also says Peter began to swear. In our present culture, we associate swearing with profanity. Peter did not use profanity. In this context, swearing was to call for a witness that he was telling the truth. When in court, witnesses swear to tell the truth, the whole truth, and nothing but the truth, and sometimes they do. Peter was calling for all to witness his denial. The strength of his denial is very surprising to us. After all, Peter was the *protos*, the leader of the twelve disciples appointed by the Lord. He always seemed so strong. How could he do such a thing to the one he said was the Christ, the

Son of the living God? What was true about Peter is true about all of us. As Matthew 26:41 says, "the flesh is weak." The things we shouldn't do, we do. The things we should do, we don't. That's a poor testimony about us, but it's true (Romans 7:13–25).

One more thing about fearful Simon Peter. Just a short time later, something in his personality changed. In Acts 4:17–18, the disciples were arrested for preaching the gospel entrusted to them in Matthew 10. They were brought before the authorities in Jerusalem and stood before the same men who condemned Jesus to death. In Acts 4:8, it says that Peter stood before them all and preached the gospel. The Sanhedrin Court was impressed, "Observing the boldness of Peter and John and perceiving them to be uneducated, ordinary men, they were amazed, and they recognized them as the companions of Jesus" (Acts 4:13). No more cringing or cowering before those who hated Jesus. Verse thirty-one says the disciples continued preaching the gospel with boldness. Persecution did not stop them. What power brought about such a remarkable change? It was the resurrection of Jesus Christ from the grave that changed them. From that point on, after he saw the risen Lord, Peter never looked back. We are not certain how Peter died, but it most likely was a martyr's death.

Does it matter what we believe about Simon Peter? If there is neither a verse in the Bible that says he was in Rome—but rather indicates that he never was—nor a verse that says he was a bishop or a pope, why believe these things? He wrote two epistles in the New Testament with no reference to any of that. He wrote only to the Jews. The Bible says he was the apostle to the Jewish people, "the lost sheep of the house of Israel" (Matthew 10:6), and never went to the Gentiles to minister except when he went to the house of Cornelius in Acts 10. The only time after that was when he went to the Gentile church in Antioch of Syria, and Paul rebuked him face-to-face before the church.

He was the apostle to the Jews and had no business in Syria, and he caused a lot of trouble there. Why didn't Peter use his power as bishop if he had it? The gospel he preached was about the Lord, Jesus Christ, coming to restore Israel's kingdom. He warns Israel about the outpouring of God's wrath during the Tribulation. The church that Paul calls the body of Christ never had or lost a kingdom, so Peter's gospel is not for us today. Israel will endure the worst suffering it has ever experienced in its history when the Tribulation, mentioned in Matthew 24, is in progress. The church, the body of Christ, will not be present on Earth, having already been delivered from the coming wrath, according to 1 Thessalonians 1:10. Does it matter what we believe about Simon Peter? Does it matter what we believe about the gospels? It matters altogether. Eternity depends on believing the truth.

CHAPTER 5
THE POPE

WHY DOES THE Roman Catholic Church have a pope? It is believed that Christ instituted this special office to represent Him when He was no longer on Earth. It is further believed that the office began with Simon Peter, whose official seat was located in Rome, Italy. However, the previous chapter on Peter gives strong evidence that he was never in Rome, was never named the bishop or head of the Christian churches and was never the rock on which Christ would build His church.

The word *pope* means "father." It has been said that it comes from the Greek word *pappas,* but this word is not found in the Greek New Testament. The word *padre* is not found either. The Greek word *pater* is the only word used for "father," and it is found over 475 times. Most times, it refers to God, the Father. Other times, it refers to birth fathers, like Zacharias was to John the Baptist; ancestral fathers like Abraham, Isaac, and Jacob; elders in the church; and spiritual fathers, like Paul was to Timothy. Never once is Peter referred to as *father*. Once, Satan, the devil, is called the father of the religious leaders in Israel (John 8:44).

The expression *Holy Father* (John 17:11) is found once and refers to God. It is never used about a man in scripture. It was only in later centuries that the expression *Holy Father* was used in reference to the pope. God's attributes were given to the pope, and it was determined that his decrees were infallible. This certainly could not be true of Peter, who issued no decrees. He repeated only what he was taught by Christ. There is no scriptural reason to believe that those said to have succeeded Peter were infallible.

By inspiration, Paul wrote, "Even if you should have countless guides to Christ, yet you do not have many fathers, for *I became your father* in Christ Jesus through the gospel" (1 Corinthians 4:15, emphasis mine). Did the church have two fathers, namely Peter and Paul? If Paul was the father of the church, where and when did he, or anyone else in the Bible, recognize Peter as the father of the church?

The Old Testament speaks of the fathers who must be divided between the founding fathers: Abraham, Isaac, and Jacob, in Acts 3:13 and Luke 1:55; and the godless fathers, called their ancestors, who abandoned God's word, killed the prophets, and led Israel astray in Luke 6:26 and Luke 11:47. Israel also had spiritual fathers, noted in Hebrews 12:9.

Jesus's words in Matthew 16 are interpreted as meaning that the pope determines the doctrines and practices of the church. "I will give you the keys to the kingdom of heaven. Whatever you bind on earth shall be bound in heaven; and whatever you loose on earth shall be loosed in heaven" (Matthew 16:19).

The kingdom referred to is Israel's millennial kingdom, which is yet in the future. It is a real kingdom on Earth and not a spiritual kingdom or church kingdom. The keys are a symbol of authority that Peter and the eleven disciples will possess when they sit on twelve thrones during the kingdom age (Matthew 19:28). Since the principal use of the keys is yet in the future, that church is also yet in the future.

The Lord will build His church during the thousand-year millennial kingdom age, and it will be a Jewish church over which Christ will rule as King of kings and Lord of lords. He will rule from

Jerusalem, and the twelve apostles will be a part of the kingdom government, occupying the twelve thrones promised to them in Luke 22:30. The Jewish church will minister to the Gentile world and bring many to Christ. The "gates of the netherworld [hades]," mentioned in Matthew 16:18, shall not prevail against the church for a good reason. Satan will be bound and cast into the bottomless pit for the entire thousand-year reign.

Without Satan's leadership and influence, those who serve him will not have the power and direction they now hold over the church. Death and the grave will not have power over believers like they will during the Tribulation because all who die for the cause of Christ will be resurrected and will enter into the kingdom age; and those who live through the Tribulation will be gathered from all nations into the promised land (Matthew 24:31–34).

The authority given to Peter by the Lord, allowing him to forgive sin, will be extended to all the apostles. This can be seen when we compare Matthew 16:19 with John 20:22–23. Matthew says, "I will give you the keys to the kingdom of heaven. Whatever you bind on earth shall be bound in heaven; and whatsoever you loose on earth shall be loosed in heaven" (Matthew 16:19). John says, "And when He had said this, He breathed on them and said to them, "Receive the holy Spirit. Whose sins you forgive are forgiven them, and whose sins you retain are retained" (John 20:22–23).

How did the apostles remit sins? They baptized repenting sinners (Jews only). That was the baptism of repentance for the remission or forgiveness of sins mentioned in Acts 2:38. It was the same as the baptism of John the Baptist (Luke 3:3). This was not a special power given only to Peter and passed on only to his successor, the second pope. It was never passed on to anyone; it was limited to the twelve apostles alone. There was no second pope. The power the apostles had on Earth will also be theirs during the millennial kingdom age.

What did Jesus mean when He said, "Call no one on earth your father, you have but one Father in heaven" (Matthew 23:9)? This verse should be taken in context with verses eight to eleven, in which the disciples and the multitude were told to call no man *rabbi*, *father*, or *master*. The acceptance of these titles shows the idea that one would feel superior to others. In view of this prohibition, one wonders why the pope is called the Holy Father. There is only one Holy Father in heaven and on Earth, and that is God, the Father.

One of the pope's duties is to spiritually feed his flock. How does he do this? Is waving his hands and pronouncing a blessing on the crowd the same as spiritually feeding the flock? When does the pope teach? Does he write books, preach from a pulpit, give seminars and lectures, or visit the many schools and universities? Where is the feed? It is said the pope is given a special grace that prevents him from leading the church into error. Where does the Bible say this? It doesn't say it. Peter was leading the church in Antioch of Syria into error (Galatians 2:11–14).

The pope is said to determine doctrines and practices. Doesn't the Bible do this completely and not need to have anything added to it? The Bible has all the doctrines we need to know. The Bible tells us how to live a life that pleases the Lord and is complete in its instructions. There is no need for a pope to add anything more to what God has said.

The two epistles of Simon Peter are infallible because every word of the original writings was given by the inspiration of God, and every word was divinely protected down through the ages of copying, translating, and publishing so that today, we can say Peter's epistles are infallible. But then, Peter was never the pope who determined doctrines and practices. He only repeated what Christ taught him.

There are also other questionable practices. For example, why do popes change their names? Why do they travel in a popemobile? Why do they live in such a luxurious palace? Jesus and His disciples never enjoyed such luxuries. Why did the church decide to relocate itself in Rome instead of in Jerusalem? Jerusalem is where the Jewish church started. How could Peter be a pope when he was clearly told by the Lord not to go to the Gentiles in Matthew 10: 5?

From what we find in the Bible, there is no scriptural reason to believe that the office of pope is a legitimate office. The only head of the church is the Lord, Jesus Christ. The Bible says so. This belief rests on the verses in Ephesians which were written after Matthew 10 and says "which he worked in Christ, raising him from the dead and seating him at his right hand in the heavens, far above every principality, authority, power, and dominion, and every name that is named not only in this age but also in the one to come. And he put all things beneath his feet and gave him as head over all things to the church, which is his body, the fullness of the one who fills all things in every way" Ephesians 1:20—23. Christ is the head of the church, not Peter or the pope. Religion has changed this idea, but God has not. The office of the pope must be rejected. Which do you believe, the scriptures or the traditions of a church? Does it matter who we believe the Holy Father is? Who is your Holy Father?

CHAPTER 6
THE PRIESTHOOD

SOME CHURCHES HAVE a priesthood. This practice may be due to the nation of Israel having a priesthood, so the imitation of it may seem like the right thing to do. In the Catholic Church, the priesthood is represented by a descending hierarchy of authority, beginning with the pope, then cardinals, archbishops, bishops, and priests. These are called *holy orders*. But there is a problem: In no way is this a copy of Israel's arrangement of priests. Israel did not have a pope, cardinals, or archbishops. Neither does this arrangement in any way represent the early church in the four gospels or in Acts. The early Jewish church had disciples, apostles, elders, and prophets. Added to this is the church called in the scriptures "the body of Christ" (Ephesians 1:22–23), with pastor and teachers, deacons, and bishops. This does not resemble the Catholic Church of today.

If it is argued that Simon Peter was the first bishop in Rome and the first in a long line of popes, and that he was the overseer of the church in Rome, then this argument needs to be challenged. The Roman Catholic priesthood is supported only by tradition, not by the Bible. In fact, the Bible refutes the idea that Simon Peter was ever in Rome or that he was ever a bishop over the Roman church.

For this argument, and to avoid redundancy, see the chapter on Simon Peter.

Simon Peter was called by the Lord to be a disciple, and later, an apostle. A *disciple* is a student, a pupil—one who sits under a teacher. An *apostle* is one who is sent by a superior on a mission. He or she receives a commission from the teacher. Although a *disciple* refers to one who is a learner, an *apostle* refers to a person who is commissioned to go forth and teach others what the apostle learned from his or her teacher. The Greek word for *apostle* means "one who is sent" and comes from the Greek verb meaning "to send." In Matthew, we read, "Then he summoned his twelve disciples and gave them authority over unclean spirits to drive them out and to cure every disease and every illness. The names of the twelve apostles are these: first, Simon called Peter, and his brother Andrew; James, the son of Zebedee, and his brother John; Philip and Bartholomew, Thomas and Matthew the tax collector; James, the son of Alphaeus, and Thaddeus; Simon the Cananean, and Judas Iscariot who betrayed him" (Matthew 10:1–4). Here, disciples and apostles do not refer to two separate groups of men, but rather to a group that is one and the same. There were disciples who were never part of the twelve (Matthew 9:14; John 6:66). Peter's commission as a disciple was to be an apostle to Israel and no one else. He was not sent to the world, to the nations, or to the Gentiles. His exclusive field of service was to the "lost sheep of the house of Israel" (Matthew 10:6). So this brings up the question, why would Peter go to Rome, a Gentile nation? It's a fair question. Peter was eager to please the Lord, and he fulfilled his commission by never departing from it.

Israel had two priesthoods: the Levitical—or Aaronic—and the Melchizedek. The Melchizedek belonged to Christ alone. Peter was never a priest and never refers to himself as being a bishop in Rome or anywhere else. No one in the New Testament ever addressed or referred to Peter as a bishop. In view of what we find and what we do not find in the Bible, it seems safe to conclude that Peter was never a bishop, had never been in Rome, and had never ministered to Gentiles—with one lone exception, which was when the Lord ordered him to go to the house of Cornelius in Acts 10.

The apostles were given power to perform miracles, forgive sins, and preach the gospel of the restored kingdom of Israel. They presented Christ to Israel as the nation's promised Messiah. The office of the priesthood ended when the following three things happened:

1. The temple in Jerusalem was destroyed in AD 70;
2. The law ended with the commencement of the ministry of the apostle Paul to the world; and
3. Israel was cast aside in Romans 9–11 and was afflicted by God with spiritual blindness and deafness according to Romans 11. With no temple in which to officiate, no law governing sacrificial offerings, and no divine program for Israel, there was no more need for priests who had no more ministry other than to preach the gospel of the kingdom.

It is important to note that the Mosaic law imposed a death sentence on anyone who usurped the office of a priest if that person was not actually a legitimate priest (Numbers 18:7). Careful genealogies were kept assuring not only the purity of the priesthood, but also the right to be king of Israel. The Lord, Jesus Christ, had rights both to be the king and a priest. Every priest had to be able to trace his ancestry back to Jacob's son Levi.

A priest should never be called *father* according to Matthew 23:9. We never read in the Bible about the Jews confessing their sins to a priest. James wrote in his epistle to the Jews, "confess your sins one to another" (James 5:16). We never read of the apostles wearing costly robes or practicing celibacy. Peter was married, and so were the other apostles. Paul wrote in the clearest terms possible, "Do we not have the right to take along a Christian wife, as do the rest of the apostles, and the brothers of the Lord, and Cephas? [Peter]" (1 Corinthians 9:5).

The Lord gave the apostles the ministry of forgiving sins. How did they do that? Was it by having the Jews come to a confessional booth to tell the priests the sinful acts and thoughts they committed? The priests forgave sins by water-baptizing people. Like John the Baptist, Jews who had faith and repented of their sins were baptized by the apostles for the remission and forgiveness of their sins. "Peter [said] to them, "repent and be baptized, every one of you, in the name of Jesus Christ for the forgiveness of your sins, and you will receive the gift of the holy Spirit" (Acts 2:38).

For a Jew who heard the gospel, believed that it was the truth, and acknowledged before God that he or she was a sinner, then this was his or her act of faith. If he or she believed the gospel that "There is no salvation through anyone else, nor is there any other name under heaven given to the human race by which we are to be saved" (Acts 4:12), then the person submitted to the act of a water baptism as a symbolic cleansing from sin. Water baptisms did not save them, but these were an outward expression of their confessions, repentance, and faith in Jesus Christ.

Today, the pope lives in one the greatest and most luxurious palaces on Earth, which is in contrast to the apostles, who lived in real genuine poverty. The Lord, not the church, provided for them according to their needs. They were instructed to make no provisions for themselves. They were subjected to physical abuse, were imprisoned, were rejected, and were ridiculed, and there is reason to believe that some, if not all of them, eventually died a martyr's death.

The only apostolic succession mentioned in the Bible is that of Matthias taking the place of the disgraced betrayer, Judas Iscariot. Matthias brought the number of apostles from eleven back to twelve. There had to be twelve apostles, no more and no less. Twelve is the number of the nation of Israel. At some point in the future, the twelve apostles will be resurrected and take their appointed places on the twelve thrones in the restored earthly kingdom that is mentioned in Luke. The Lord said, "And I confer a kingdom on you [twelve], just as my Father has conferred one on me, that you may eat and drink at my table in my kingdom; and you will sit on thrones judging the twelve tribes of Israel" (Luke 22:29–30).

The apostle Paul did not succeed anyone. He was raised up by the Lord for a separate and distinct ministry. When the apostle James was killed, he was not replaced like Judas was. This was an indication that a new, divine program was beginning, in which the twelve apostles would have no part. As far as the record shows, they never departed from their original commissions in Matthew 10. Peter exercised no apostolic authority over Paul. He did not teach Paul the gospel of the grace of God; it was the exact opposite. Paul taught Peter and the other apostles the gospel that he received directly from the Lord. It was different. They neither knew nor had ever heard Paul's gospel before he taught it to them. A quick-but-studious glance at Galatians 1–2 will confirm this.

When Peter visited Antioch of Syria, Paul faced him publicly and accused him of duplicity. Peter had no business in Antioch and caused some serious problems by going there. He was proselytizing Gentiles to Judaism. Peter's ministry was to the Jews, not the Gentiles in Antioch. If his presence in Antioch of Syria caused problems, what would his presence in Rome have done?

In view of all the above, it seems safe to declare that what today is called the priesthood is far from anything we find in the Bible. It should not be regarded as anything but religion and never should be trusted or relied upon for anything. The scriptural order for today is for the church to have pastors and teachers, not priests. It would be out of order to follow Peter when we should follow Paul. This is another important issue in which it matters what we believe.

The Roman Catholic Church has practiced celibacy for priests and has forbidden marriage for nuns for centuries. In the beginning, this was not the case. Historians cannot trace the practice of celibacy back further than the fifth or sixth century AD. The doctrine and practice of celibacy has left many Roman Catholic men and women unfulfilled and lonely.

Celibacy does not honor God. It goes against the plans and purposes of God, who created men and women with a basic need for companionship. God said, "It is not good for the man to be alone" (Genesis 2:18). It is the first thing that God said was not good. When did celibacy become good, and who changed God's purpose? Why is it good for Roman Catholic men and women? Is celibacy and the denial of basic needs a sacrifice that brings glory to God?

Marriage supposedly hinders serving God. Since humans were created with a strong sexual desire, marriage provides the means for satisfying that burning drive. God inspired Paul to write, "It is better to marry than to be on fire" (1 Corinthians 7:9, cf. verses 28 and 36). Without marriage, humans will find a way to satisfy their drive, and the result will be sin and shame. Marriage brings order to how humans are to live together. Adam and Eve were ordered to bear children and to populate the earth. Companionship, sexual satisfaction, and bearing children are denied to priests and nuns. Many parents urge a son or daughter to become a priest or a nun. They are so proud to have their child assume such an office. This is so sad when we think of the many children who do this only to satisfy their parents.

Love is a need and a wonderful experience. Research has shown that babies who were born but never loved often died from something called *moroseness*. Moroseness comes from a lack of love. The babies who experienced this were rarely picked up, kissed, cuddled, talked to, or shown affection. Love is one of humanity's basic needs. Nuns and priests never give or receive this type of love because they do not marry. They experience family love and the love of friends, but not romantic love. Love between spouses is more intimate and binding than any other human love.

Forbidding marriage is an indication of false religion according to 1 Timothy 4. Some religions, for spiritual reasons, "forbid marriage and require abstinence from foods that God created" (1 Timothy 4:3). This is a serious matter. Verses one and three speak of religions whose teachings are the doctrines of demons and of seducing spirits.

Demons and seducing spirits are under the supervision of Satan. Some doctrines are hypocritical lies. God says so. Forbidding people to marry might be a leading cause of sexual sins among the clergy. They are robbed of the joys of marriage spoken of in the Bible.

We read in Proverbs, "to find a wife is to find happiness, a favor granted by the Lord" (Proverbs 18:22). Wise King Solomon wrote, "Enjoy life with the wife you love, all the days of the vain life granted you under the sun. This is your lot in life, for the toil of your labors under the sun" (Ecclesiastes 9:9). And, by the way, wouldn't there be more Catholic children born in the world if priests and nuns could marry? The burden on Catholic couples to have more children would perhaps be lessened. There would be less pressure on sons and daughters to become priests and nuns. If priests could marry, then they would be better able to council married couples who need spiritual advice and guidance. The old saying is still true, it takes one to know one!

So, how are we to understand the Bible passages that say not to marry? There are some biblical commandments forbidding marriage. For example, the Jews were forbidden marriage to Gentiles. The instructions Paul mentions in 1 Corinthians 7 give a good commentary on this subject. First, fornication is sin between unmarried people. Fornication is condemned and forbidden. "But because of cases of immorality, every man should have his own wife, and every wife her own husband" (1 Corinthians 7:2). How much is *every*? That's God's solution to the sin of fornication. Why should God's solution be changed?

It is believed that the apostle Paul, before he was converted, was once married and that his wife died. He was widowed. If he married again, it would have been a burden for him and his new wife because of the intensive schedule he had in carrying the gospel to the world. A wife would have suffered with him. He recognized that some men had the gift of living without being married. In 1 Corinthians, which was originally inspired word-for-word by the Lord, Paul wrote, "Indeed, I wish everyone [widow and widower] to be as I am, but each has a particular gift from God, one of one kind and one of another" (1 Corinthians 7:7).

In Mathew 19, the question of divorce arose. The disciples wanted to know why Moses gave some Jews the right to divorce. The Lord replied that in the beginning it was not so, but the Israelites had sinned and disobeyed the Lord concerning marrying Gentiles. Israel was God's people, and He wanted them to keep themselves separated from the Gentiles, who were religious idol worshipers. To marry a Gentile would introduce paganism into a Jewish family. If many Jews married many Gentiles, it would not be just the families contaminated, but the nation. It would defeat the purpose that God had in separating Abraham from his idol-worshipping family. Jews would become contaminated by their spouses' pagan worship.

God knows how to fix problems. If a Jew married a Gentile, the only way to prevent pagan religions from affecting Jewish families was to divorce the Gentile spouse. It was the only way to correct the problem. When the disciples heard this, they said, "If that is the case for a man with his wife, it is better not to marry [a Gentile]" (Matthew 19:10). Do not marry a Gentile, and there will be no pagan influence and no need for divorce.

There are some men who are gifted to remain single. For example, eunuchs do not usually marry. Some men are born eunuchs and some are made eunuchs; but when it is done by choice, such celibacy is a self-determined gift. Priests are not eunuchs. God says in His Word, "Let marriage be honored among all and the marriage bed be kept undefiled, for God will judge the immoral and adulterers" (Hebrews 13:4).

Does it matter what one believes about celibacy and marriage? It has mattered to many men and women who were deceived into thinking it was a good-and-right thing to do. Enforced singleness has led to lives of loneliness and unhappiness. It's a feature of Catholicism that ought to be abandoned. Celibacy has never been necessary; God is not pleased with it. It is unnatural and unscriptural, the father of many problems, and it does matter what we believe about it.

CHAPTER 7
TRANSUBSTANTIATION

TRANSUBSTANTIATION IS THE belief that when the bread and wine are received in a communion service, the elements are literally changed into the flesh and blood of the Lord, Jesus Christ. This explanation is taken from the *C. I. S. Extension Course*, based on the Confraternity of Christian Doctrine, revised edition of the *Baltimore Catechism*, number 3. It can be found in this extensive doctrinal statement, but can it be found in the Bible? The Catholic Church thinks it can.

In book five of the *Baltimore Catechism*, chapter 26 is entitled "The Holy Eucharist." It is stated that the Holy Eucharist is a sacrament and a sacrifice. In the Holy Eucharist, under the appearances of bread and wine, it says, "the Lord is contained, offered, and received. The whole Christ is really, truly, and substantially present in the Holy Eucharist" (*Baltimore Catechism*, number 343). We must ask, is this true? It is the understanding among most churches that the bread and wine only represent the body and blood of Christ, and that Christ is literally in heaven seated at the right hand of the Father. How can Jesus Christ be here on Earth in the Eucharist and in heaven at the same time? Many find the idea of eating human flesh and drinking human blood repulsive.

In the Bible, it was called the Last Supper because it was evening and was to be the last meal Jesus would eat with the disciples before He was crucified. The crucifixion would take place the following morning. At this meal, He took the bread, blessed it, and gave it to His disciples, who passed it around and each took a piece. Jesus said to His disciples, "Take and eat; this is my body" (Matthew 26:26). He also took a cup of wine, blessed it, gave it to His disciples, and said, "Drink from it, all of you, for this is my blood of the covenant, which will be shed on behalf of many for the forgiveness of sins" (Matthew 26:27–28).

The Last Supper is recorded in the three synoptic gospels: Matthew 26:26–29, Mark 14:22–25, and Luke 22:14–20. Then He told them, "do this in memory of me" (Luke22:19). Those who reject the Catholic interpretation also observe the Lord's Supper, believing that the purpose is to recall and remember that Jesus Christ died to be our Savior. He shed His blood, by which our sins are washed away once and for all time, never to be recalled.

To practice the partaking of the bread and drinking of the wine, thinking that it must be done to sacrifice Christ anew, is to also believe that His sacrifice on the cross at Calvary was insufficient and incomplete and must be repeated over and over. Christ died and was made alive by the Holy Spirit of God. He is alive in heaven right now. How can He be alive in heaven and dead on Earth at the same time?

The word *Eucharist* means "thanksgiving." The Catechism says that a person can have everlasting life by partaking of the Eucharist. Does the Eucharist have the power to impart spiritual life to a sinner and to restore such a person to a right relationship with the Lord? If Jesus partook of the bread and wine at the last supper, did He receive everlasting life?

If the bread and wine change in form to the body and blood of Christ, can anybody see this change take place? If not, how would anyone know a change has happened? If the answer is that it must be taken by faith, then is this the proper use of our faith? What it boils down to is whether we should take the words of the Lord, Jesus Christ, literally or figuratively.

The Bible expressly forbids the consumption of human blood or eating of human flesh. Moses warns the Israelites, "Not one among you, not even a resident alien, may consume blood" (Leviticus 17:12). Moses made the warning much stronger: "You shall not consume the blood of any flesh" (Leviticus 17:14). Since the life of all flesh is in the blood, anyone who consumes it shall be cut off from God's people or have any relationship with God. This same commandment is repeated in other places in the Bible, such as Leviticus 19:26, Deuteronomy 12:16 and 12:23, and 1 Samuel 14:31–34. The Lord's disciples decided at the church conference in Jerusalem to warn believers against consuming blood (Acts 15:20 and 15:29).

The shed blood of the Lord, Jesus Christ, is to be remembered for what it does for us. Drinking real blood does nothing. Paul wrote, "whom God set forth as an expiation, through faith, by his blood, to prove his righteousness because of the forgiveness of sins previously committed" (Romans 3:25). He taught the Ephesian believers that "we have redemption through His blood" (Ephesians 1:7). Hebrews supports Ephesians, saying, "Without the shedding of blood there is no forgiveness" (Hebrews 9:22). Colossians says, "And through him to reconcile all things for him, making peace by the blood of his cross" (Colossians 1:20). Ephesians 2:13 says that we have "become near [to God] by the blood of Christ." Romans 5:9 says, "We are now justified by His blood." Luke wrote, "The church of God that he acquired [purchased] with his own blood" (Acts 20:28). These are some of the things that Christ's shed blood has done for us. Drinking communion wine does none of these things for us. It only reminds us of these things that the blood of Christ does as the Lord's supper was meant to do.

It is said that Christ had the power given to Him to change the elements from bread to His literal body and to change wine into literal blood. Matthew 28:18 is quoted as proof that He was given this power. There are two Greek words for power, *exousia* and *dunamas. Exousia* means power in the sense of authority. Kings have power. *Dunamis* means power in the sense of strength, might, ability, and capability. Samson had strength.

These two words convey completely different meanings. Matthew was saying that all authority and governing power will be given to Him at the Second Coming when He shall establish Israel's kingdom and David's throne. Christ will be given all power to rule and to occupy that throne as the King of kings and Lord of lords.

It is said that only ordained priests have the power to change the bread and wine into the body of Christ. The power was given to them in the sacrament of the Holy orders. It is said that Christ made the apostles priests at the Last Supper when he said to them, "Do this in memory of me" (Luke 22:19). The priests exercise this power when they officiate in the mass.

Christ's body was meant to bear our sins (1 Peter 2:24). His body was subjected to terrible torment at the hands of the religious leaders in Jerusalem and by the Roman soldiers stationed there who nailed Jesus to the cross. The sacrifice of Himself as the Lamb of God was a one-time occurrence, not something to be repeated. Peter says, "For Christ also suffered for sins once, the righteous for the sake of the unrighteous, that he might lead you to God. Put to death in the flesh, he was brought to life in the spirit" (1 Peter 3:18).

We are to worship a living Christ, not one who is dead and who is being constantly sacrificed. Rather than being present in a wafer, He is, at this very moment, in heaven, seated at the right hand of God, the Father. Christ is present in His children here on Earth by His spirit that indwells all believers in the Lord, Jesus Christ (Romans 8:9).

At the Last Supper, in Matthew 26:29, He tells His disciples that He would *not* be present with them again until the kingdom of God, also called the kingdom of heaven, is established here on Earth. If He was not going to be with them again until the kingdom age, how could He be present in the wafer and wine at this present time? Is it true that Jesus also partook of the bread and wine? Did He consume Himself?

It makes more sense to follow the scriptures than an unnatural religious interpretation on this matter. There are too many problems with the teaching of transubstantiation to consider it a true doctrine. To say that we believe it by faith is insufficient. Too many times, faith has been misplaced. Having faith in wrong conclusions does not change them into right conclusions.

What is the difference between blind faith and superstition? Christ instituted an observance that we might remember His death, burial, and resurrection. We are prone to forge or minimize the importance of His death, burial, and resurrection. The broken bread represented Christ's body that would be physically broken, even as bread is broken. Though not a bone in His body was broken, His flesh was severely torn.

Bread symbolized life, and wine symbolized death—the life and death of Christ. Christ said, in reference to the bread, "This is my body." The verb *is* means "represents." For example, we read, "The field is the world" in Matthew 13:38. Was the field the world, or did the field represent the world? King David wrote, "Your word is a lamp for my feet" in Psalm 119:105. *Your word* refers to the Bible, God's Word. Is the Bible a literal lamp that sheds literal light? Of course not, but it is God's instruction that sheds light on how a believer should walk.

Light stands for knowledge and understanding. "The harvest is the end of the age," noted in Matthew 13:39, means that the harvest represents the end of the world. "The rock was Christ," mentioned in 1 Corinthians 10:4, means that the rock represented Christ. By the same token, the Lord said, "This is my body," meaning that the bread represented His body. Since Christ was present with His disciples, He could not have meant that the bread was His body too.

How could the bread be His body when He was seated there with them? It was a figurative expression like that in Matthew's gospel, when the Lord said to Simon Peter, "Get behind Me Satan" (Matthew 16:23). He did not mean that Peter was Satan; it was a figure of speech. At the Last Supper, it was not conceivable that Christ would hold His own body in His hands and then break it to be consumed by His disciples. There was reference to only one body present, not two. It is not the real presence of Christ in the wafer but the absence of it. To believe that the bread and wine are changed into Christ's literal body and blood contradicts—with all scientific tests applied—the evidence we see. It seems that if the bread and wafer are changed and become Christ, then they ought to be worshipped because they become God. This would be false worship.

In his book *The Lord's Supper,* Cornelius Stam makes an important point.

> We had always considered the word "this" to be a pronoun (a word used in place of a noun to avoid redundancy) referring in this case to the bread and wine. Indeed, in each record of this incident it is clearly stated that our Lord took the bread and the wine and said, "Take it, this is my body" (Mark 14:22). Had he said, this has now become My body, it might be possible to accept the doctrine of transubstantiation but, according to Rome's own insistence that is means is, we conclude that it was the bread which He called His body, i.e. as representing it.[2]

If this is not the correct interpretation of His words, then what about Luke's more complete record, where the Lord says, "This cup is the new covenant in my blood" (Luke 22:20)? First Corinthians 11:25 says the same thing. Perhaps sacramentalists will explain how a cup can become a covenant. The Roman Catholic translation of

---

[2] Cornelius Stam, *The Lord's Supper,* 22.Berean Bible Society, Chicago, *IL, 1981*

the Bible has no footnote to explain this. Obviously, the cup and its contents represented the new covenant.

Another important fact in this connection is that in the Greek and Hebrew, the substantive, *to be*, is not expressed when dealing with simple matters of fact. Thus, in some Bible versions in the rendering of Paul's statement, "All scripture is inspired by God" (2 Timothy 3:16), the *is* appears in italics. This indicates that the word was supplied by the translators and is not found in any known Greek manuscripts. But when a symbol or figure of speech is intended, the word *is* must be used. Thus, in the phrase, "the field is the world," the word *is* does appear in Greek, as it must. The appearance of *is* in our Lord's words about the bread and the cup indicates that He was using a figure of speech, meaning that the bread and the wine represented His body and blood.

Did the disciples think they were eating Christ's flesh and drinking His blood while they were at the table with Him in full view? By partaking of the bread and the cup without hesitation or question, it appears they understood that the bread and wine only represented Christ's body and blood. There is nothing in the record that indicates they adored either of the elements. Paul says in 1 Corinthians 10:16 that it was the communion of the bread and cup that directed one's attention of worship toward the Lord. That's what it was meant to do.

If Christ taught that He would literally be present in the bread and wine, how could the disciples have continued to believe that when they saw Him ascend into the heavens? Can partaking of the bread and wine give a person everlasting life? Judas Iscariot was present with the disciples at the Last Supper. He partook of the bread and wine. Did he receive everlasting life at that time? Can bread and wine serve as mediators between a sinner and Christ Jesus just because a person partakes?

It seems that there are three dangerous errors in religious teaching today that came out of the Dark Ages:

1. apostolic succession;
2. the official duties of a supposed priesthood that has the power to transform elements; and
3. the dependence on sacraments as an essential channel of grace.

The Jewish Passover was not a solemn occasion but was instead a joyful festival. It celebrated deliverance from bondage. Before Christ died on the cross and shed His blood, sins were atoned for by the blood of animals offered by faith in sacrificial offerings. When Christ died, that changed. His bloodshed did what the blood of animals could not do. *Atonement* means "to cover." Christ's blood does not cover our sins; it does something far better. It takes our sins away.

At some time during the week, we place our garbage out at the curb to be picked up by Waste Management, who takes it away. We will never again see the garbage they take away; it will never be returned to us. This is a permanent arrangement. We do not want the garbage back. It is taken away, gone forever, and forgotten. That's what the shed blood of Christ does for sinners. By shedding His blood, our sins are taken away, gone forever, never to be remembered by God.

The Lord said, "This cup is the new covenant in my blood, which will be shed for you" (Luke 22:20). Was the cup transubstantiated into a covenant, or did it stand as a symbol? Transubstantiation was declared a dogma, and a curse was pronounced upon all who denied the doctrine of the real, literal presence of Christ in the bread and wine. This makes it very hard for a person raised in Catholicism to reject this teaching, no matter how difficult it is to believe or how many statements of scripture contradict it.

The sacrifice of Himself as the Lamb of God that takes away the sins of the world was a one-time occurrence that cannot be repeated—and neither does it need to be. Peter says, "For Christ also suffered for sin once, the righteous for the sake of the unrighteous, that He might lead you to God" (1 Peter 3:18). Being offered once was sufficient; it was enough. No more sacrifice was necessary. After He was crucified, Christ was made alive, a living Christ—not one who is continually sacrificed—and He is alive and in heaven today (1 Peter 3:18–22).

In Matthew 26:29, the Lord plainly said He would not be present with the twelve disciples again until after He returns and establishes the kingdom. When Jesus partook of the elements, did He eat His own flesh and drink His own blood? The following passages in the NABRE forbid the drinking of blood: Numbers 23:24, Deuteronomy 12:23 and 15:23, 1 Samuel 14:32–34, and Leviticus 17:12. Now, if the Bible expressly forbids consumption of literal flesh and blood, why would the Lord instruct the twelve and all others after them to drink His blood? Does the Lord not keep His own laws? Would the Lord teach His disciples to disobey the scriptures? The shed blood of Christ was for the remission of sins and does not have to be consumed to be effective. It is the blood of Christ that makes men nigh unto God and brings peace between a sinner and the triune Godhead. To check this out, go to these passages in the Bible: Colossians 1:20, Ephesians 2:13, Romans 5:9, and Acts 20:28.

In the New Testament, bread was used to symbolize the union of the members of the church, the Body of Christ: one bread, one body of believers (1 Corinthians 10:17). The bread also symbolized fellowship with Christ. At the Last Supper, the bread was most likely Passover bread, unleavened. Can a wafer represent Passover bread? The church never had a deliverance from an enemy like Israel had deliverance from Egypt, passing over the Red Sea on dry land. Why is it that bread is distributed to the laity and the wine is withheld? The twelve drank the wine. The churches in the New Testament epistles drank the wine. When God inspired His words to be written down, did He foresee the misrepresentation of the bread and the wine and address this matter beforehand? Although the Passover commemorates Israel's deliverance from bondage to the

Egyptians, the Lord's Supper commemorates the sinner's deliverance from the penalty of sin and bondage to sin, which is an even greater deliverance (Romans 6:23).

In the church, which Paul calls the body of Christ, the partaking of the bread and cup in a communion service is an observance without any superstition attached and will continue to be a practice until the Lord appears in the clouds of heaven to take the body of Christ out of this world. The Lord's death should not be regarded as a martyrdom, but rather as a necessity for putting away our sins forever. Paul says in 1 Corinthians 5:7, "Christ is our paschal lamb"—literally, He is our Passover, which means His death serves as our deliverance.

Christ called Himself a "stone" (Matthew 21:42); a "vine" (John 15:1); a "gate" (John 10:9); and "the bread" (John 6:48–51). Was He literally a stone, a vine, a door, or bread? Are these not symbolic terms? By the same token, the bread and wine were figurative, not literal. Wine and wafers remain literal unchanged wine and wafers. When the Lord, Jesus Christ, died on the cross as the Lamb of God who takes away the sins of the world, He was not literally a lamb; but he died like a lamb being sacrificed. Search the scriptures to see whether these things are so. We owe it to ourselves to make sure that we believe the truth. In the end, it will matter what we believed and may determine where we spend eternity.

The world seems incurably religious and superstitious. No matter how farfetched and absurd teachings and beliefs may be, they are accepted without question or investigation. Little thought is given to whether they make sense or seem right and, most of all, whether they are contradicted by the Word of God. For many people, if the church says so, that's good enough for them. If the preacher says so, it must be right; he ought to know. But God has given us adequate intelligence to think these matters through. It behooves us to use our God-given abilities to weigh our beliefs carefully. It matters what we believe.

CHAPTER 8
THE SACRIFICE OF THE MASS

WHAT IS THE celebration of the mass? According to the *Baltimore Catechism*, lesson twenty-seven, book five, it's the sacrifice of the new law in which Christ, through the ministry of the priest, offers Himself to God in an unbloodied manner under the appearance of the bread and wine. Mass means dismissal.

What is a sacrifice? It's the offer of a victim by a priest to God alone, and the destruction of it in some way to acknowledge that He is the Creator of all things. It is the most perfect way for people to worship God.

The principal priest in every mass is Jesus Christ. The priest is a secondary minister. It is essential that, every day, two hundred thousand masses are said around the world. Since the elements become the literal blood and body of Christ, it seems that Jesus suffers the terrible agony of the crucifixion endlessly. Fundamental Christians do not understand the celebration of the mass because of what the scriptures say. They believe the Bible refutes the celebration of the mass. What scriptures do fundamental Christians have in mind that cause them to deny the observance of the mass?

First, Hebrews 7–10 offer the following explanation: "so also

Christ, offered once to take away the sins of many, will appear a second time, not to take away sin but to bring salvation to those who eagerly await Him" (Hebrews 9:28). If we do not force a meaning upon this verse, it sounds like Christ offered Himself once for our sins. However, if the bread and wine are literally changed into Christ, how can we escape the thought that Christ is being offered again and again, about two hundred thousand times every day?

Second, "He [Christ] has no need, as did the high priests, to offer sacrifices day after day, first for their own sins and then for those of the people; he did that once for all when he offered himself" (Hebrews 7:27). Does this verse imply that there is no need for Christ's sacrifice day after day, but that His sacrifice of Himself— once, for all time and all sinners—is all that is needed? That's the impression it leaves. There is no need for daily repetition.

Third, "But this one offered one sacrifice for sins, and took his seat forever at the right hand of God" (Hebrews 10:12). It sounds like this verse is saying that Christ's one-time offering for our sins would be effective forever.

Fourth, "he also says: "Their sins and their evildoing I will remember no more." Where there is forgiveness of these, there is no longer offering for sin" (Hebrews 10:17–18). God sacrificed His Son once for our sins, venial and mortal. This verse says there is forgiveness and no more need for an offering for sin. If our sins are completely forgiven once and for all, is there any need to suffer in Purgatory? What sins would one pay for if one's sins, past, present, and future, are completely forgiven? Where in the Bible does it say sins are only partly forgiven?

Fifth, "But if we walk in the light as he is in the light, then we have fellowship with one another, and the blood of his Son Jesus cleanses us from all sin" (1 John 1:7). Does all mean all, or does it need to be qualified? If Christ's blood, shed and offered once for all, took away all sin once for all, why is there any need for the mass?

Those who are saved from the wages of sin are those who have taken God at His Word, believed in the Lord, Jesus Christ, and trusted in His finished work on the cross—where the sin problem was solved, paid for once for all time and eternity, and with no religious works of any kind being required for salvation. The only works ever required for our salvation were God's works. That's what seems clear enough from the passages quoted above.

A search by scholars and students of theology has not been able to find anything in the written records of church history, where the mass was celebrated before AD 1215. If others object and say that this is not true because Christ celebrated the first mass the evening before His crucifixion, then this needs to be challenged as to whether the Last Supper can really be considered a celebration of the mass. At the Last Supper, where was all the ritual and pageantry of today? If it wasn't present then, why is it present now? Were the elements really transformed into the literal body and blood of Christ while He was standing before His disciples? This is an extremely strange doctrine, indeed!

When Christ died on the cross, He cried out, "It is finished" (John 19:30). What was finished? All that needed to be done to save a lost soul, providing complete forgiveness of sins to "everyone who believes" (John 3:16), who has believed in Christ and His finished work of salvation. God will give everlasting, never-ending life to every person who will believe in His work through Christ. Christ's death was completely sufficient in every respect. Religion refuses to believe in a salvation such as this and includes its own religious works that some believe will help save themselves. They go the way of Cain and bring damnation to their own souls. Religion insists on doing more—and sometimes less—than what God asks or requires. People insist on their own input as though the salvation of their souls is incomplete unless they personally add something to it.

Salvation is so simple. "And they said, 'Believe in the Lord Jesus and you and your household will be saved'" (Acts 16:31). Paul and Silas told the Philippian jail warden how he and any member of his house could be saved from the awful wages of sin: just simply by believing in the Lord, Jesus Christ. What does it mean to believe in the Lord, Jesus Christ? It means to believe everything God, the Father, has said about Jesus Christ in the Bible, as much light as one has, and to trust in everything God has done through Christ to provide salvation to all who believe. It matters what one believes about the celebration of the mass.

CHAPTER 9
THE CHURCH

THERE ARE SO many kinds of religions and churches around the world, it is bewildering for someone who wants to know what is right. There are people interested in knowing the truth and who believe it is important to know what and who is right. How can one be sure what to believe? Each religion and church believes it teaches the truth and stakes the eternal destiny of the soul on its beliefs. With whom should a person affiliate?

How has it happened that all these different belief systems came into the world? We have a reliable ancient record that unfolds the historical beginning of world religions. We also have the most expert authority on the subject whose knowledge can be trusted. God is the highest of all authority; He knows absolutely everything. He also can pass on perfect information to those He has created. He has done this by placing His words in humankind's minds and guiding them in writing down ancient history, reaching all the way back to the beginning of creation. Because of the authorship of the Bible and God's wisdom and ability to reveal truth to humanity, the Bible can be fully trusted to teach us the truths on which we can rely. The

Bible tells us how religion began. This unadulterated account from God is not contaminated with humans' thoughts, words, or ideas.

God did not need people's help to say what He wanted to say. Not only is "all scripture inspired by God" (2 Timothy 3:16), it is also preserved by His power over the centuries so that today, we can still regard it as God's Word and not people's. If God can create the universe with the planet Earth among the hosts of heaven, why should it be hard for God to inspire a word-perfect Bible to be written and then preserve what He inspired? He really wants us to know the truth. He wants us to know how religion began and became diverged from the truth.

Because there are so many different belief systems, this tells us that somebody is wrong; they have to be. Paul's words in his letter to Pastor Timothy support the above statements, saying, "All scripture is inspired by God and is useful for teaching, for refutation, for correction, and for training in righteousness, so that one who belongs to God may be competent, equipped for every good work" (2 Timothy 3:16–17). In the beginning, mankind knew the uncorrupted truth (Romans 1:18–25).

Religion began just outside the gate of the garden of Eden, perhaps even before the inhabitants of the garden were expelled from the garden. After Adam and Eve committed the sin of disobedience, they were ushered out and denied access to the garden. They covered their nakedness with fig leaves, but God stripped away these coats and made them a set of clothing acceptable to Him. We learn from this that humans try to do things to make themselves presentable before God, but it never works. God made them clothes from the skins of slain animals, most likely lambs, and from this we learn that, to stand before God, we must be clothed in that which God provides for us.

Adam and Eve learned that the sacrificial offerings of lambs were the only acceptable means of faith and worship, and all other means of worship would be rejected. Anything else would be the same as making coats of unacceptable fig leaves. A sacrifice in which a lamb would be slain, and its blood sprinkled on the offering, would be the only act of faith and worship that God would accept.

Cain, the firstborn son of Adam and Eve, brought an offering to the Lord. Cain was a "tiller of the ground" (Genesis 4:2); in other words, he farmed. He brought the fruit of the harvest to the God in whom he believed. Cain's offering was rejected. Abel, Cain's brother, was "a herder of flocks" (Genesis 4:2); he was a shepherd. He sacrificed an unblemished lamb and sprinkled its blood on an altar. This was his worship (Hebrews 11:4, 12:24). Abel's offering pleased the Lord; God accepted it. We learn from this, however, that not all forms of worship are acceptable to God.

It's God's way or no way. He makes no exceptions. Cain was given a chance to repent and to bring a proper offering to the Lord, but he would not change his ways of worship. At this point in time, humanity became fatally religious. Religion is false worship unless God states otherwise. Judaism, the religion of Israel, was a worship system of dos and don'ts. God established it.

Religion is a form of worship of dos and don'ts, a system that believes in God or a god, and that God rejects just like He did with Cain's offering. Man's do was a don't. Just as Cain refused to change his errant worship system to that made known by God, people today will not abandon their religions for the Christian faith set forth in God's Word.

People love their religions with all the formalities and pageantry. They think God also loves all this. "Sometimes a way seems right, but the end of it leads to death" (Proverbs 14:12). This does not keep God from offering salvation to "everyone who believes in him," according to John 3:16. Out of a heart of great love, He refuses to give up on us. It cost God the Father way too much, in giving His Son, the Lord, Jesus Christ, to save lost sinners like us, for Him to quit now.

Religion is not acceptable to God. The true church, we are told, is in Rome, directed by the Catholic bishops in union with the pope. This is a serious claim that needs to be disputed. If it is the true church, it ought to be able to pass the tests of the true church. Did Jesus start a church while He was here on Earth? Does the Bible say He did? If it does, it seems like it ought to say it not just once, but many times. This point would be too important to be mentioned only one time. Where is the one time it's mentioned? It's not found even once.

What does the word *church* mean? Studies of the Greek language of the New Testament indicate that the word means "a called-out assembly." The Greek word is *ekklesia*, a compound word consisting of a preposition and a noun or a verb. Greek-language manuals tell us the preposition is *ek*, which means "out of." The Greek word *Klesis*, a noun, or *kaleo*, a verb, is translated as "a calling" or "to call." So the church, the *ekklesia*, is "a called-out assembly."

The word is used in the Bible to refer to a body of people called together for a specific purpose. It is used with reference to both godly and ungodly people. In Acts we read, "Meanwhile some were shouting one thing, others something else; the assembly [*ekklesia*] was in chaos, and most of the people had no idea why they had come together" Acts 19:32. It is describing a riot by unbelieving Ephesians. The same word, *assembly*, is used again in verse thirty-nine.

Elsewhere, the word *ekklesia* is translated as "church." There is a reference in Acts when Stephen was addressing the deeply religious Sanhedrin Council, that said, "It was he who, in the assembly [*ekklesia*] in the desert, was with the angel who spoke to him on Mt. Sinai and with our ancestors, and he received living utterances to hand on to us" Acts 7:38. The ancestors were the Israelites, and the wilderness was the Arabian desert. Israel was referred to as an assembly (*ekklesia* in the *Septuagint*), who were called out of Egypt by God under the leadership of Moses, who received the law on Mt. Sinai.

Israel was being led to the promised land, namely Canaan. We note in Acts 7:38 that the same people were called the assembly in the desert in the Catholic Bible and were composed of both believers and unbelievers. Many died in unbelief on their forty-year journey to the promised land. The trail they followed was like one long cemetery. They were most certainly an interesting Old Testament church. The New Testament book of Hebrews is a commentary of Israel's sins and troubles in the wilderness.

Five different assemblies (churches) are identified in the New Testament:

1. Israel in the wilderness: one time, in Acts 7:38.
2. The church in the four gospels that assembled at the temple and in the synagogues: three times, in Matthew 18:17.
3. The church that Paul called in his epistles the body of Christ: sixty-eight times, in Romans 16:1.
4. Assemblies of unbelievers: three times, in Acts 19:32.
5. The millennial church that Christ will establish at His Second Coming: one time, in Matthew 16:18.

The body of Christ is mentioned many more times than the other four churches put together. Interestingly, this church is mentioned only by the apostle Paul and is therefore found only in his epistles. But if Jesus Christ founded a church while here on Earth, shouldn't this be recorded in the four gospels repeatedly? A church is mentioned twice in Matthew 18:17. The only other reference is found in Matthew 16:18, and the Roman Catholic Church stakes its claim on this verse. Matthew 16 and Matthew 18 are speaking of two different churches. Since we dealt with the passage in Matthew 16 in the chapter on Simon Peter, it would be redundant to go over it again here. The church in Matthew 16 is the future millennial church. The church in Matthew 18 is the past Jewish church in Bible times.

The Catholic Church did not exist when Christ was on Earth; neither did it begin with Him. The Catholic Church did not exist at the time Paul wrote his epistles, so the body of Christ cannot be the Roman Catholic Church—neither did the body of Christ ever become the Roman Catholic Church. It came into being when those in the body of Christ diverged into a separate entity in later centuries.

By divine inspiration, Paul wrote these words in Ephesians 1:22–23: "And he [the Father] put all things beneath his feet [Christ's] and gave him as head over all things to the church, which is his body, the fullness of the one who fills all things in every way." This body is composed of all the people—beginning in Acts 13 and continuing to the present—who have received Jesus Christ as their Savior, be they Jew or Gentile. A person can join a local church and not be a member of the body of Christ. Many people have their names on church membership rolls but have never received Christ as their personal Savior.

Church membership is not a savior. When a sinner receives the Lord, Jesus Christ, into his or her heart, something amazing happens. The Holy Spirit of God takes up residence within that person. If the Bible did not say this, we would not believe it. "But you are not in the flesh; on the contrary, you are in the spirit, if only the Spirit of God dwells in you. Whoever does not have the Spirit of Christ does not belong to him" (Romans 8:9). In 1 Corinthians 3:16, we read, "Do you not know that you are the temple of God, and that the Spirit of God dwells in you?."

The indwelling of the Holy Spirit is called the installment of the Spirit in 2 Corinthians 1:22. A better word for *installment* would be *earnest*, which means "a guarantee" or "a brand mark showing ownership." Cattle are branded with registered brand marks showing who owns them. The sinner who received Christ as his or her Savior is bought with a price, and that person belongs to God. God knows who belongs to Him by the brand mark—that is, His Spirit, which indwells all who are His children. God cannot be fooled about who His children are.

It is true that the founder of the church, the body of Christ, was the Lord, Jesus Christ. But He did not found the church during His earthly ministry; He founded the church after His death, burial, and resurrection through the raising up of the apostle Paul. The body of

Christ made its initial appearance somewhere in the middle of the book of Acts after Paul's conversion. In fact, a whole new historical chapter began with Paul that is commonly called the age of grace or the dispensation of grace. It is also called the church age.

The Old Testament prophets received revelations from God that the Messiah would be born and that He would die for their sins, be raised from the dead, and would later reestablish Israel's lost kingdom. One of the things not revealed to the prophets was the name of the Messiah. When the Messiah came, He was born as the prophets said and grew into manhood, but no one could tell by looking at Him that He was the Messiah. He could say that He was the Messiah, but saying so doesn't make it so. He looked like any other Jewish man walking down the streets of Galilee and Judea. There would be no halo about His head, no special Messianic toga, and no special speaking voice.

How, then, were the Jews to know that Jesus of Nazareth was Israel's promised Messiah? One piece of proof was that He fulfilled the genealogical requirements by belonging to the right nation (Israel), the right tribe (Judah), and the right family (David's). His name, *Jesus*, means "savior." He was born where the prophets said the Messiah would be born, in Bethlehem of Judea.

The thing that singled Him out and proved that He was Israel's Messiah was the miracles. He would do things no other man could do; miracles were His credentials for the office of Messiah. Jesus's miracles fulfilled prophecy. He said, "Believe me that I am in the Father and the Father is in me, or else, believe me because of the works themselves" (John 14:11). When John the Baptist presented Jesus Christ to the Jewish nation, the Jews learned for the first time the personal name of their Messiah. He was Jesus of Nazareth, the Lord from heaven; He was Emmanuel, God with us. He was the Lamb of God who would take away the sins of the world. The Jews who heard John the Baptist acknowledged that Jesus was their Messiah and believed in Him became members of the Jewish church in Israel, a church that lived strictly under the Mosaic law.

The church that began with the ministry of John the Baptist was growing, and so was opposition to it and to Jesus personally. But what about the miracles? The Jews credited Jesus's miracles to "the power of Beelzebul, the prince of demons" (Matthew 12:22–24). How terrible! The scriptures were set aside, and false doctrines took their place. It is hard to prove anything about the Lord, Jesus Christ, or the church, if the Bible is ignored or rejected. The Bible is God's record of Christ. The rabbis and Pharisees in Israel must take full responsibility for misleading the Jewish nation with false doctrines and religious philosophy, or, as the Bible calls it, "human precepts" (Mark 7:7). This has not changed; it is still the pattern today. What Cain did in the beginning, the scribes, rabbis, Pharisees, and teachers in Israel also did. If it was wrong for them to do it, then why should it be thought right for anyone to do the same today and to think it doesn't matter?

Where does the Bible say that Jesus started or founded a church? A church is composed of people who believe the gospel. People believed the gospel preached by John the Baptist, so why would that not constitute a church? The believers were Jews called out from among an unbelieving Israel. A church already existed when Jesus began His ministry. Where does the Bible say that salvation depends on joining a church? People join churches because they are saved, not to be saved.

Churches are not saviors. The only Savior is Jesus Christ. Where does the Bible say that one human man was designated to be the Holy Father of the church? We have shown in the chapter on Simon Peter that he could not have fulfilled this role; neither was the church built on him. The only Holy Father mentioned in the Bible is God Himself.

On the first page of the *C. I. S. Extension Course*, it says that the traditions of the church can be proven by common sense alone. What is *common sense*, and how trustworthy is it? The dictionary defines *common sense* as "sound, practical, good judgment." It amounts to what people think about this, that, and the other thing. There is something far more trustworthy than common sense or what people think—namely the Bible, God's Word. We trust it for what it says rather than for what it does not say. We need to know what God says about this, that, and the other thing.

Tradition has been accepted by many as being on equal authority with the Bible. It may sound good and right, but Proverbs 14:12 says, "the end of it leads to death." The death mentioned in this verse means separation from God. Now, that's serious. A true church and a true believer never go beyond the Bible; it is God's complete and infallible word. Christ alone is the head of the church, which is the body of Christ. The church needs no other head. Christ is "the beginning, the firstborn from the dead, that in all things, he himself might be preeminent" (Colossians 1:18).

The church is not the door to Christ. It is just the opposite; Christ is the door to the church. We become members of the church through Christ alone. The early church was never under the administration of the priesthood. The twelve disciples or apostles were the Lord's witnesses and teachers, and they were never priests. It matters what you believe about the church because you might belong to the wrong church and believe its false teachings.

CHAPTER 10
BAPTISM

THE DOCTRINE OF baptism has confused the church for ages. The cause of the confusion is simple: people follow traditional beliefs rather than the Bible. Fundamental Protestants are as confused and divided as everyone else. The doctrine of baptism is not confusing in the Bible. It's not God's fault that people do not understand it. When God inspired the Bible to be written, He included rules on how it is to be studied and understood. One of the rules is that the Bible is to be rightly divided into its proper parts. God inspired Paul to write, "Be eager to present yourself as acceptable to God, a workman who causes no disgrace, imparting the word of truth without deviation" (2 Timothy 2:15). When the Bible is rightly divided, it makes it less complicated and more easily understood. Wrong division is deviation and leads to a hodgepodge of confusion and wrong application that nobody can explain.

There is another reason for confusion about baptism. Some of the things taught today are not actually in the Bible. These things have been invented, created, and imagined, and they have no biblical foundation whatsoever. The Bible is set aside, ignored, and replaced by the made-up commandments of churches and theologians.

Baptism is not a New Testament doctrine. It was instituted by Moses, acting under God's specific directions. The priests serving Israel under the Aaronic priesthood, beginning with Aaron and his sons, had to be washed with water, which symbolized cleansing. This was done at the entrance to the tabernacle and was their initiation ceremony into the priesthood. Why did John the Baptist baptize Jesus? This marked the beginning of Jesus Christ's office of priestly ministry, who would offer Himself as the Lamb of God that takes away the sins of the world. Jesus did no miracles until He was baptized and anointed by the Holy Spirit.

Baptism, or washing, was not only a symbolic cleansing; it also represented humble service. In the New Testament, the Lord washed His disciples' feet, an act of humble service. He baptized their feet. When Simon Peter declined to have Jesus wash his feet, Jesus said, "Whoever has bathed has no need except to have his feet washed, for he is clean all over; so you are clean, but not all" (referring to Judas Iscariot in John 13:10). Service without humility is not acceptable to the Lord.

God created the nation of Israel to be "a people for his name," as noted in Acts 15:14, among the pagan Gentile nations. They were to live separate from the Gentiles but, at the same time, be a witness and testimony to all nations. Israel was to be a light to the Gentiles. "I, the Lord, have called you for justice, I have grasped you by the hand; I formed you, and set you as a covenant for the people, a light for the nations [Gentiles]" (Isaiah 42:6). Listen to Peter's description of Israel. "But you are a chosen race, a royal priesthood, a holy nation, a people of his own, so that you may announce the praises of him who called you out of darkness into his wonderful light" (1 Peter 2:9).

The Jews were to have a priestly ministry to the world. But first, they had to repent, be baptized, washed, and made clean for this ministry. Thus, we read in Acts 2:38, "Peter [said] unto them, repent and be baptized, every one of you, in the name of Jesus Christ for the forgiveness of your sins; and you will receive the gift of the holy

Spirit." Israel was not a clean nation. Before they could serve God as a light to the Gentile nations, they needed to repent and be baptized, washed, and cleansed. Unfortunately, though some responded to the call of the twelve disciples, the majority rejected their ministry. It would do well to remind ourselves here that their ministry of baptizing was for Jews only. Israel was the only priesthood nation.

When Jesus was baptized, He fulfilled all righteousness. John thought he should not baptize Jesus because John's baptism was for the remission of sins. Jesus had no sin, and John apparently knew this—but not all baptisms are for the remission of sins. Jesus needed to be baptized "to fulfill all righteousness" (Matthew 3:15). What does that mean? We read in the Old Testament, "This is our justice [righteousness] before the Lord, our God: to observe carefully this whole commandment he has enjoined on us" (Deuteronomy 6:25). The Lord's commandments included the order of the priesthood, including the initiation ceremony of induction into the office. So Jesus's reply to John was that it was necessary to fulfill all righteousness by following the law He came to fulfill. Jesus's baptism made his priesthood ministry legitimate.

When we ask how many kinds of baptisms are mentioned in the Bible, we often hear two, three, or four at the most. In fact, there are twelve. Here is a list of the twelve baptisms with their scriptures.

Water Baptisms (Wet):

1. The divers water baptisms of Judaism, (Hebrews 6:2 and 9:10), were ritual washings.
2. Traditional Jewish water-baptism ceremonies that Christ condemned (Mark 7:1–7).
3. John the Baptist's water baptism of repentance, (Luke 3:3).
4. Christ's water baptism (Matthew 3:13–15).
5. Pentecostal water baptism for Israel (Acts 2:38).

Baptisms Not Related to Water (Dry):

1. Israel's baptism unto Moses (1 Corinthians 10:1–4).
2. Christ's baptism unto death (Luke 12:50 and Mark 10:38–39).
3. Noah's typical dry baptism (1 Peter 3:20–21).
4. Baptism for the dead (1 Corinthians 15:29).
5. The baptism of fire (Matthew 3:11).
6. The baptism of the Holy Spirit, who places a sinner into the church, the body of Christ when he or she receives Christ as Savior (1 Corinthians 12:13).
7. The Holy Spirit's baptism of supernatural power (Luke 24:49 and Acts 1:4–5).

In view of these baptisms, we read in Ephesians 4:5 that there is "one Lord, one faith, *one* baptism." But why does it say *one* if there are *twelve*? It is because, for the church, the body of Christ, there is only one baptism that is necessary. Which of the twelve baptisms is it? It is the baptism of the Holy Spirit noted in 1 Corinthians 12:13. When a sinner receives Christ as his or her Savior, the Holy Spirit immediately places that person into the church, the body of Christ, as a member of the body. This baptism has nothing to do with water; neither are we taught that water is to be used to symbolize it. It is often referred to as Holy Spirit baptism.

A pastor friend who was asked what he believed about baptism gave this explanation: He admitted that what he believed and practiced was not in the Bible, but it was a necessary practice to keep the church pure. Does a water baptism have the power to create purity in the church? When we think about it, we wonder just how pure the churches are that practice water baptisms. What's wrong with teaching doctrines that are not in the Bible? Just about everything. There is plenty wrong, and seriously so. It deceives people. It's what religion does.

Making up a teaching usually results in its being passed off somehow as scriptural. If not that, then it is made to sound spiritual and therefore assumed to be correct. But the other side of the coin is that it makes the Bible incomplete. Those who make up doctrines are saying, in effect, that God did not complete His task and that He needs humanity's help in making all truth known. He can't do His work without us. Isn't making up doctrines the same as adding to the scriptures, a practice soundly condemned several times in the Bible? Isn't making up doctrines the same as tradition?

Mark 7:1–16 makes it abundantly clear that unscriptural doctrines are wrong, dangerous, and condemned by God. The Pharisees had a doctrine of baptisms they called *washings* (the Greek word is *baptizmos*), which they made up. Notice the Lord's judgment of this practice, "In vain do they worship me, teaching as doctrines human precepts" (Mark 7:7). That's clear enough. There is no need for an interpretation. What happens when humans invent doctrines? Jesus explains, "You disregard God's commandment but cling to human tradition" (Mark 7:8).

Everything God wants us to know about baptism is in the Bible and needs no additional teaching; neither should anything be taken away from what God has revealed. God does not need to be corrected or to be helped by people providing further information, as though God has not said enough. So, my friend was wrong in thinking that teaching something unscriptural about water baptisms would in any way be accepted by God or be helpful to the church. If it was wrong for the Pharisees to do it, it is equally wrong for us to do it today.

In the Confraternity of Christian Doctrine, *Baltimore Catechism* number three, lesson twenty-four, it says, "Baptism is the sacrament that gives our souls the new life of sanctifying grace by which we become the children of God and heirs of heaven. By means of sanctifying grace received in baptism we are spiritually reborn." It also says, "After His resurrection, Christ commanded all to receive baptism as a necessary condition for salvation." It then goes on to say, "Baptism takes away original sin." And "baptism takes away both eternal punishment ... and temporal punishment on earth or in purgatory. By baptism ... we become members of the church." If all this is true, then who needs the Lord to save them? None of these Catechism statements are true. Water baptisms are powerless to impart anything spiritual to a soul. The Bible does not say any of these things. They are all the inventions of the authorities of the church.

The Catholic Church teaches that children are to be baptized as soon as possible after birth, at which time they are given the name of a saint and have him or her for a protector. This practice promotes superstition. It is never stated which of the twelve baptisms is practiced here; neither is any mention ever made of rightly dividing the baptisms for proper understanding and application. This is because they do not know there are twelve baptisms.

Does it matter what you believe about baptism? If a person trusts baptism to deliver him or her from hell or from anything here on earth or in Purgatory, that person is in for an unpleasant surprise. His or her sins remain, and judgment is certain. It may matter for all eternity what a person believes about baptism.

CHAPTER 11
THE BIBLE

THE COUNCIL OF Trent (1545–1548) declared that there were two equal sources of divine truth: namely, the Bible and tradition. This declaration was confirmed by the Vatican Council (1962–1965). In the Roman Catholic Church, the Bible and tradition are of equal importance. This marks a great difference between Catholics and most Protestants. So much of what the Catholic Church teaches is based on tradition that the Bible is unintentionally relegated to an inferior position. The Catholic Church will undoubtedly deny this, but the Bible fades into the background.

Two things worth noting are:

1. Catholics are not urged to read the Bible, though the church quotes it often. Many have been told that the Bible is too hard to understand because it is the mind of God and that ordinary reader needs to be told what it means. The church says they need professional help with this, like the help of a trained clergy. As one Catholic was told, "You don't have to read the Bible. We will tell you what to believe."

2. Catholics know much about their traditional theology but little about the Bible. It causes outsiders to wonder what Catholics are taught about the Bible since traditional doctrines seem to be far more prominent. It stands to reason, if one does not read the Bible, then his or her knowledge would be naturally limited.

To many fundamental Protestants, the Bible is regarded as the Word of God. More than that, it is the inspired Word of God. This conclusion comes from the Bible's own testimony about itself; it says it is the Word of God from cover to cover. It says that all scripture is given by the inspiration of God (2 Timothy 3:16) and that God breathed His own words into the minds of all the biblical writers. They neither added to nor subtracted from what God said; we have the pure words of God in black and white.

Additionally, many Protestants believe that, in order to assure unending accuracy, God protected His words from corruption—not only in the original autographs, but in the thousands of copies and the various translations with innumerable printings. Though there are hardly two ancient manuscripts that are exactly alike, somewhere among them, God's inerrant word is there. It's the job of textual criticism to search out the words. If God can create the universe, the planet Earth, and all things on it, it would have been easy for God to author a book like the Bible.

The Bible is God's Word in a sense that there is no other book like it. It is especially unique. It was inspired in a way that no traditional writings are. The Bible opens itself to investigation and encourages its readers to examine the scriptures to see what is so (Acts 17:11). This is what the Bereans did and were considered honorable in doing so. In contrast, traditional doctrines cannot be investigated by searching the scriptures, history or much of anything else.

God gives us rules for biblical investigation. For example, Paul told Timothy to rightly divide the scriptures because he knew it would be impossible to understand the Bible without dividing it. Wrong understanding could lead to the damnation of a soul.

God had a plan for saving sinners, which was formed before Adam was created. God made this wonderful infallible plan because, by His foreknowledge, He knew that humanity would sin and would need a Savior. From the beginning of the Bible to the last pages, the message is about a Savior who would come into the world for all sinners. On this point, the Bible is divided into four parts:

1. In the Old Testament, the message is about the Savior, sent by God, who would come into the world.
2. In the four gospels of the New Testament, the message is about the Savior, sent by God, who came into the world.
3. In the book of Acts and the Pauline epistles, the message is about the formation of the body of Christ, the church of which Christ is the head, and for whom He will return to escort it to heaven.
4. In the rest of the Bible, the message is about Christ, who will come again, sent by God at the Second Coming, with judgment and the restoration of Israel and her kingdom. From cover to cover, the Bible is about the person and the work of God through His Son, Jesus Christ, the Lord from heaven.

The Bible makes it clear that humanity is dependent on God, its Creator; on Christ, the sinner's Savior; and on the work of the Holy Spirit. Though God wants us to do good works, no matter how good and prolific they may be, they cannot save us. Good works are not saviors. People cannot enter the presence of God in heaven by their own personal merits. They cannot enter heaven unnoticed; that is to say, they cannot sneak into heaven hidden among the crowd of saints marching in. They cannot get into heaven by joining a church.

God offers us salvation as a gift; receiving it is up to the sinner. The act of believing in the person and the work of the Lord, Jesus

Christ, is the way a sinner receives the gift of salvation. Believing in Christ is all God asks of us. Some think that is too much, and others say that is too easy. Why would anyone want God's plan of salvation to be harder? If a person can't respond to His offer when it is so easy, what makes anyone think he or she will respond if it is harder? God has deliberately made it easy to be saved.

The Bible is composed of sixty-six books, written by many writers over fifteen hundred years. There was almost no collaboration between the writers, yet the theme of the Bible remains the same: it is about the Lord, Jesus Christ. The Bible does not speak of inspired men; it speaks of inspired scriptures. The writers were God's scribes, and their pens were God's pens. There is no way to prove that the traditions of Catholicism were inspired by God.

One of the many things noticeably absent from traditional theology is prophecy. The Bible is not only filled with prophecy; it also records the fulfillment of it. We can be totally confident that the prophecies not yet fulfilled will be at some point in the future. Fulfilled prophecies and the miracles recorded in the Bible are strong evidence that the Bible is God's Word and not humanity's. Prophecy is truth made known to the biblical writers who were moved by the Holy Spirit. Peter, inspired by God, accurately reports, "Know this first of all, that there is no prophecy of scripture that is a matter of personal interpretation, for no prophecy ever came through human will; but rather human beings moved by the holy Spirit spoke under the influence of God" (2 Peter 1:20–21). The word *moved* means "to be moved along like a leaf being carried along by a little stream of flowing water." The leaf does not move by its own power, but rather, by a force not its own. The Holy Spirit was the power that moved people to write down God's words, completely omitting any words of their own.

According to Hebrews 1:1–2, God spoke through His Son. Jesus said He spoke only the words of His Father as He taught the disciples and the multitudes. "The word you hear is not mine but that of the Father who sent me" (John 14:24). Jesus taught the Old

Testament "beginning with Moses" (Luke 24:27), who wrote the first five books of the Bible. Moses and the prophets prophesied about Christ. It was not the writers whom the Lord emphasized— He only mentioned four by name; instead, it was the messages they prophesied.

The prophets did not always understand what they wrote, but they knew they were writing God's Word. Over two thousand times, we find expressions like "thus says the Lord," beginning in Exodus 4:22, or "then God said," beginning in Genesis 1:3. King David, the writer of Psalms, said, "The Spirit of the Lord spoke through me; His words were on my tongue" (2 Samuel 23:2). The prophet Jeremiah said, "The word of the Lord came to me" (Jeremiah 2:1). The writer of Hebrews wrote, "In times past, God spoke in partial and various ways to our ancestors through the prophets; in these last days, He has spoken to us through a [the] son [Son] whom he made heir of all things and through whom he created the universe" (Hebrews 1:1–2).

The Lord, Jesus Christ, referred to the Old Testament writers often because He knew they wrote God's words. He referred to Moses frequently. What did Moses say? What did Moses write? What did Moses command? The Lord never once told His listeners to look for future doctrines that would become the traditional teachings of the church. Paul wrote to the church in Colossae, "of which I am a minister in accordance with God's stewardship given to me to bring to completion for you the word of God" (Colossians 1:25). His epistle brought the writing of the Bible to its conclusion. Paul, not John, was the last to write scripture.

When Paul wrote 2 Timothy, that was the last time God spoke. He has not spoken or moved anyone to write since then. Paul also wrote, "This God has revealed to us through the Spirit" (1 Corinthians 2:10). The Bible is the voice of God—every book, chapter, word, syllable, and letter. Tradition is the voice of people and contains no provable revelations from God. The Lord said, "You search the scriptures, because you think you have eternal life through them; even they testify on my behalf" (John 5:39).

The Bible is called God's Word, not because He spoke every word—because, in fact, He didn't speak every word. Some words are the words of kings, jailors, robbers, and religious people. Some words are spoken by Satan. The Bible is called the Word of God because He inspired every word to be written, whether the words are His or the words of someone else. God knew perfectly well what others said and quotes them perfectly. For His own purposes, He wants us to know what others said. The New Testament writers were never accused of tampering with the scriptures of the Old Testament; they simply believed it was God's Word.

Making traditional church doctrines equal authority with the Bible implies that the Bible is insufficient by itself. Traditional teachings were added by the church to supplement the Bible. This is a serious error, for which the church is responsible. The Bible is not subject to the church; it is the exact opposite. The church is subject to the Bible. To be subject to the Bible is to be subject to the Word of God. The apostle Paul wrote to Pastor Timothy, "and that from infancy you have known [the] sacred scriptures, which are capable of giving you wisdom for salvation through faith in Christ Jesus" (2 Timothy 3:15). This was written long before traditions were added. The Bible was already sufficient for the most important thing in a person's life, namely, the salvation of a soul.

Holy men of God, who were qualified by the infusion of the breath of God, wrote in obedience to the divine command and were kept from error, whether they wrote down truths they were already familiar with or newly revealed truths. To say that the Bible is marred is to say that God has failed to guard His Word. Traditional doctrines do not agree with the Bible. If traditions said what the Bible says, then they would not be tradition; they would be commentary on the Bible. This is what the Reformers saw. Even when traditional doctrines seem to have Bible verses supporting them, they don't. Quoted verses are misunderstood, wrongly interpreted, and misapplied. The traditional doctrine of transubstantiation is a case in point.

One never hears in Catholic teachings about the mystery of which Paul wrote so often and for which he suffered so much. What Paul wrote became the traditions of the early church. The scribe who wrote the book of Hebrews does not mention tradition. "Indeed, the word of God is living and effective, sharper than any two-edged sword, penetrating even between soul and spirit, joints and marrow, and able to discern reflections and thoughts of the heart" (Hebrews 4:12).

Everybody ought to read the Bible, love it, be led by it to salvation, and walk in the light of its instructions. Everybody ought to look for a church to attend that is a Bible-only church, where, from it pages, its inexhaustible truths are constantly taught.

The Bible should never take a back seat to traditions because these are open to fair investigation. The scriptures are by far more certain, more permanent, and not subject to change. The Bible shows the awesome wisdom, omnipotence, and omniscience of the Creator of the universe. It is more credible because it can be checked and has great authority behind it.

Does it matter what we believe about the Bible? Tradition is not a lamp unto our feet or a light unto our pathway, but the Bible is all that and more. Speaking by inspiration of God, David said, "Your word is a lamp for my feet, a light for my path" (Psalm 119:105). Does it matter what we believe about the Bible being God's Word, a lamp, and a light on our pathway to salvation and heaven?

CHAPTER 12
THE SAINTS AND SAINTHOOD

TWO BROTHERS WHO were born and raised in a church that emphasized honoring the saints, attended a wedding in a Protestant church. They had never been in such a church before and were surprised to see that there were no saints on the walls or on the stained-glass windows. They didn't know that the saints gathered every Sunday and sat in the church pews instead.

According to the Roman Catholic Church and the *Baltimore Catechism*, lesson seventeen, a saint is someone officially declared by the church to be in heaven who may be publicly venerated by those here on Earth. Veneration is an act of respect and honor. Saints are said to be honored by people imitating their holy lives; by praying to them; by showing respect to their relics or bones, pictures, clothing, souvenirs; and by having images of them, such as statues, and portraying them on stained-glass windows.

Statues and pictures are forbidden only when they are used to promote false worship. All this is taught by tradition, but in the Bible, the first of the Ten Commandments makes statues and pictures a sin, especially those of a deity. According to the Catholic Church, saints in heaven have the power to hear when they are prayed to and have intercessory power. They go to God with the prayers of people on Earth.

The word *saint* is mentioned nearly a hundred times in the Bible—thirty-eight times by Paul alone in his epistles. The word is found four times in the singular form in the Old Testament and thirty-five times in the plural. It is found only one time in the four gospels, but it is found seventeen times in the books from Hebrews to Revelation. The first mention is in Deuteronomy 33:2–3, where the Hebrew is translated as *holy ones*, the same being true of the last mention, in Revelation 20:9. With this context to examine, a great deal can be learned about saints, or the holy ones.

How do Catholic beliefs and practices about saints stand when compared to the Bible? We know from the Bible that saints can be living either here on Earth or in heaven. Matthew 27:52 is a difficult passage to explain, for it says that when Christ died and was resurrected, some of the saints who had already died rose from their graves and went into Jerusalem. Those who knew them must have been shocked beyond belief to see them and wanted an explanation. The Bible does not give us any more information about them; it only leaves us to wonder.

In Acts 26:10, Paul testifies about his life before he became a believer. He says that he shut up many of the saints and holy ones in prison. Again, Paul addresses his epistle to those in Rome, who were called saints in the church. Romans 1:7 says that the saints were "called to be holy [saints]."

In some versions of the Bible, the verb *to be* is in italics, which means there was no known manuscript that contained this verb in that verse in Greek. The honest translators wanted us to know they inserted the verb to make the verse clearer. That the translators succeeded is debatable because the verse became more muddled than clear. Romans 1:7 says the Christians in Rome were called *holy* or *saints*. Who called them holy saints? Since God inspired Paul to use this phrase, it was God who called them holy.

Why did God call the Christians saints? When a lost sinner turns to the Lord, Jesus Christ, for salvation, in the very first moment of belief, he or she becomes a child of God. At that time, God gives the new believer an identity. He calls the person a holy saint. God is good at picking names and titles. When Jesus was born, neither Mary nor Joseph picked a name for Him. God's angel told them to name their newborn baby. "You are to name him Jesus" (Matthew 1:21). Why Jesus? The same verse goes on to say, "For He shall save His people." *Jesus* means "Savior."

Every person, place, and thing has a name by which it is identified. The Greek word for *saint* is *hagios*, which means "holy or holy one." Holiness is not earned; it is credited by God for every believer in Christ. It is not used in the Bible to refer only to those who exhibit exceptional holiness. In 2 Thessalonians 1:10, believers are described as holy ones or saints. Angels are called holy beings because that's the way they were created, not because of some special acts or holy deeds they did. God's Spirit is called the Holy Spirit not because of holy acts it performed, but because holiness is the very nature of God the Spirit.

Likewise, Christians are called saints or holy ones because God made holiness a part of their spiritual nature, which, in turn, makes believers fit to enter God's presence. The Christian's holiness has nothing to do with the acts or deeds committed by the believer; rather, the believer's behavior should display holiness. There are no references to saints being prayed to in the Bible; no references say they can hear the prayers of people on Earth. There are no references saying they can intercede before God for people on Earth in any way. Paul says in Romans 8:26–27 that it is the Holy Spirit who intercedes for us: "In the same way, the Spirit too comes to the aid of our weakness; for we do not know how to pray as we ought, but the Spirit itself intercedes with inexpressible groanings. And the one who searches hearts knows what is the intention of the Spirit, because it intercedes for the holy ones (saints) according to God's will."

The Holy Spirit is our intercessor. In fact, the saints on Earth often depended on other believers for help. The Christians in Rome were directed to "contribute to the needs of the holy ones. Exercise hospitality" (Romans 12:13). The saints needed help; they were not giving help. That the saints in heaven have no ministry to or for anyone on Earth must be a great disappointment to those who trusted in them. Saints minister to each other here on Earth, which is why Paul said in Romans 15:25–26, "Now, however, I am going to Jerusalem to minister to the holy ones. For Macedonia and Achaia have decided to make some contribution for the poor among the holy ones in Jerusalem." For more information about this, see also 1 Corinthians 16:1–2, and Paul's words in 2 Corinthians 9:12.

If saints were the holy beings that some claim, then they would not need to be reminded of the necessity of living a pure life as in Ephesians 2:19. It is not the saints in heaven who are to pray for us; it is the saints on Earth who are to pray for the saints on Earth. The role of the believers is expressed this way: "With all prayer and supplication pray at every opportunity in the Spirit (Ephesians 6:18). Praying for one another is part of the ministry of the saints in the body of Christ (1 Corinthians 9:11–12).

There will come a day when all the saints—that is, the members of the church called the body of Christ—shall be joined together. Those who are on Earth will be with those in heaven. This will happen when the Lord appears in the clouds to call the body of Christ out of this world to take them to heaven (1 Thessalonians 4:13–18).

The statements mentioned above have not been taken from church catechisms, church doctrines, church councils, or the like. These statements are all from the Bible, which carries more weight than all the church decrees put together. God's Word stands as the first and final authority for what we believe. Every believer is a saint—not because he or she has have lived a holy life, for, it's sad to say, some have not. The believers in Corinth were saints, but many of them did not live holy lives. Every believer is a saint because God, by His grace, has blessed the believer with unmerited holiness. Holiness is a gift from God. Every child of God is blessed with holiness, without which he or she cannot stand in God's presence. When it comes to a matter of beliefs and practices, it matters what we believe about holiness, saints, and sainthood.

CHAPTER 13
PURGATORY

MANY ASSUME THAT there is a difference between Protestants and Catholics about where the soul goes after death. There are some differences between them, but these are not as great as some think. Both believe that the departed soul goes to a real place. Both believe that there are at least three real places beyond our planet Earth— namely, heaven, hell (*sheol*/Hades), and the lake of fire. However, Catholics have another place they believe in, called Purgatory. What is Purgatory? Is it a real place? What goes on in Purgatory?

The soul of every human being goes somewhere after death. Fundamental Christians believe that the soul of a believer in the Lord, Jesus Christ, goes directly to heaven, entering immediately into the presence of Christ. They believe that their sins have been completely forgiven and that there is nothing left to pay for. Christ paid sin's debt in full, and believers' appropriation of forgiveness— past, present, and future—are realized the moment a person receives Christ as his or her Savior.

This position is denied by Roman Catholic theology. Fundamental Christians believe that all unbelievers who die without repenting of their sins will go to hell and will eventually be resurrected to stand before the great white throne for final judgment. They will be condemned and cast into the lake of fire for all time and eternity.

According to www.dummies.com, the Catholic Church teaches that Purgatory has two purposes. The first is that the departed dead must suffer temporary punishment for sin committed after baptism. The second purpose is for the cleansing from the attachment of sin.

Time in Purgatory purifies the soul before entrance into heaven. A soul is purified by fire, making Purgatory like a minor, reduced, or inferior hell. This teaching became prominent around the eleventh century and was confirmed at the Council of Trent. In contrast, fundamental Protestants believe that we are cleansed by the shed blood of Christ, not by our own suffering in Purgatory. John wrote that the blood of Jesus Christ "cleanses us from *all* sin" (1 John 1:7, emphasis mine). This is supported by many other biblical references.

How can a soul get out of Purgatory? There are two means of escape. Those living on Earth can pray for the dead, offering an indulgence. During the Middle Ages, indulgences were so abused that it helped to pave the way for the Reformation. No one knows when enough prayers have been said or when enough masses for the dead have been observed to help a soul get out of Purgatory. No one knows when enough indulgences have been paid. Do people pay money for the dead at these masses? The Reformers like Luther and Calvin taught the doctrine of justification by faith. They said that when a soul is converted, a person is immediately justified and declared righteous by God. At death, the soul goes directly to heaven, and there is no need to pray for that person.

The scriptures quoted to support the doctrine of Purgatory do not mention such a place. Second Timothy 1:16–18 says that Paul hoped the Lord would bless his good friend, Onesiphorus, with mercy "on that day." Catholicism teaches that the "day" refers to time in Purgatory. By the furthest stretch of the imagination, it cannot be made to mean that. "That day" refers to "the judgment seat of Christ" noted in 2 Corinthians 5:10, which will take place in heaven when rewards are issued to believers for their good works.

In Matthew 12:32, the expression "the age to come" is said to refer to Purgatory, but again, this is a misunderstanding of what Matthew said. "The age to come" is a reference to the time when Israel's kingdom will be restored at the Second Coming of Christ.

Luke 16:19–26 is the story of the rich man and the beggar, Lazarus. A rich man died and awakened in hell. He was in torment from the flames. The *New American Bible* translates the Greek word *Hades* as "netherworld" (Luke 16:23). Hades was divided into two parts: one part was where the righteous went when they died, which, in Luke, is called *Abraham's bosom* and is also called *paradise* in Luke 23:14. The other part was simply called *Hades* in Greek, and that was the abode of the unrighteous. It is a place of fire and torment. This is the place the Catholic Church calls *Purgatory*. No one is said to have passed from the torment side of Hades to the paradise side of Hades or to have gone to heaven. A great gulf between the two sides prevented a soul from passing from one side to the other.

In 1 Corinthians 3:11–15, we have a more difficult problem. Fundamental Christians believe it is talking about the Lord's workers, who build on the foundation that is Christ Himself. They built doctrines on this foundation. These doctrines are taken from the Bible, are correct, and will be rewarded.

Those whose doctrines are not correct will not be rewarded. They will suffer the loss of reward although they themselves will be saved. The teacher will not be destroyed, but his erroneous doctrines will. This will take place at the judgment seat of Christ, the reward seat for Christians in heaven. The judgment will take place in a short period of time. The use of the word *fire* likely does not refer to literal fire, but rather is a figure of speech in the scriptures, like the use of the fig tree or the olive tree. Though teachers taught false doctrines, they were believing Christians, or else they would not have appeared before the reward seat of Christ in heaven.

The writer of Hebrews supposedly referred to Purgatory. All it says is, "For our God is a consuming fire" in Hebrews 12:29. How does that indicate there is a place like Purgatory? Purgatory denies that Christ's death was completely sufficient in forgiving our sins. With this belief, Christ's death and His bloodshed are considered only a partial payment for sin.

Since "all have sinned" (Romans 3:23), it stands to reason that all must suffer in Purgatory. The Catholic Church calls this "the particular judgment." Those who have been baptized and go to Purgatory to pay for the unforgiven sins that they committed after being baptized and never confessed are certain of heaven as soon as God's justice has been satisfied. Those guilty of mortal sins do not go to Purgatory; they go directly to hell. Heaven and hell are forever; life on earth and Purgatory are temporary.

In many countries, there is an observance called All Saints' Day. It is held in commemoration of all the saints who have died, both the known and the unknown. In the United States we celebrate something like it called Halloween. Many who celebrate Halloween have no idea what it's all about. Fundamental Protestants do not observe All Saints' Day, but Catholics observe it on November 1st as a remembrance of those who are in Purgatory.

The Catholic Church teaches that Purgatory is necessary because Revelation 21:27 says nothing unclean shall enter God's presence in heaven. Fundamental Christians believe that we are made clean by the blood of Christ. Nothing in Purgatory can make us clean. It's the blood of Christ that makes a sinner clean, not suffering in Purgatory. Matthew 12:32 does not teach that a person who dies in his or her sins can be freed from the penalty of sin after death. Does it matter what we believe about how our sins are dealt with that will determine where we will spend eternity?

CHAPTER 14
THE HOLY CITY

MANY RELIGIONS IN the world have holy cities. For example, Judaism has Jerusalem in Israel, the Muslims have Mecca in Saudi Arabia, and Roman Catholicism has the Vatican City in Rome. Of special interest in this chapter is the comparison between two of these holy cities: Jerusalem and Rome.

Vatican City is a country in itself, a city within a city. It is an ecclesiastical state, an enclave of Rome. It is the seat of the Roman Catholic Church and has been located there since about the seventh century. It has worldwide authority over all Catholics.

The government of Vatican City is an absolute monarchy with its head being the pope, who also serves as its king. Because it is a monarchy, it cannot be accepted into the European Union (EU)— an entity made up of twenty-seven nations on the continent of Europe—for economic and political purposes. To be a member of the EU, it is required that a country be a democracy.

Vatican City is mostly surrounded by a wall that has six entrances, but only three of which are open to the public. Its population numbers about a thousand people—the majority being men, with only a small population of women. Many of the men are

ELVIN C. MYERS

priests, and many of the women are nuns. There are a few men and
women who are civil servants, however. No one is born in Vatican
City because there is no hospital. The laypeople are engaged in
secretarial, domestic, trade, and service occupations.

Vatican City has residential dwellings, museums, art galleries, the
world's largest library, a daily newspaper, and a radio and television
station. The most impressive structure is St. Peter's Basilica, which is
built on the supposed grave of the apostle Peter. Construction on the
basilica began in the fourth century. The Vatican even has a football
team—or soccer, as it's called in the United State, a phone system,
a banking system, a pharmacy, gardens, a railway, a post office with
its own stamps, its own license plates, a national anthem, and a flag.
It also owns a telescopic observatory in Arizona in the United States.

Vatican City has embassies in many countries, but there is not
one in itself. It is one of the wealthiest entities in the world with
assets estimated between fourteen and fifteen billion dollars. It
levies no income tax. It receives its income from contributions from
its church members all over the world. It has investment holdings
estimated to be around 1.5 billion dollars. It also receives income
from the sale of coins, stamps, and from its many publications. Its
banking operations and expenditures have been made known to the
public since the 1980s.

Jesus said, "Foxes have dens and birds of the sky have nests, but
the Son of man [Jesus] has nowhere to rest His head" (Luke 9:58). In
contrast, the pope lives in the spacious, luxurious Apostolic Palace in
Vatican City, and he also has a summer residence in Alban Hills. He
is the absolute head of the Roman Catholic Church and is referred
to as the Holy Father. He is guarded by the Swiss Guards, who are
carefully chosen Swiss men. They have served in this capacity since
AD 1506. The Vatican government has been called the Holy See
since 1929, with the pope being its bishop.

All the city's supplies that support its population and its activities
must be imported. Interestingly, Vatican City is one of the largest
consumers of wine among the European countries. It also has one

of the largest crime rates, likely due to the many tourists who visit the city every year.

The above is a brief resume of Vatican City. It stands in contrast to Israel's cities, Jerusalem and Bethlehem. Rome is considered the city of Simon Peter. Jerusalem and Bethlehem are the cities of David.

Jerusalem is a very ancient city that was made the capital of Israel by King David when he took it from the Jebusites. Just about five miles south is the little town of Bethlehem, where David was born (Luke 2:4 and 2:11). Both places are called the city of David, but only Jerusalem is called the holy city.

Rome is mentioned nine times in the Bible and is never called a holy city. Jerusalem is mentioned 829 times and is called the holy city many times. The first time it is so called is in Nehemiah 11:1, and then again in 11:18. It is also called a holy city In Isaiah 48:2 and 52:1, as well as in Daniel 9:24, in the Old Testament. In the New Testament, it is called the holy city in Matthew 4:5 and 27:53, and in Revelation 11:2, 21:2, and 21:10.

If Simon Peter resided in Rome as the first bishop and wrote two epistles, then surely he would have mentioned at least one time that he lived there and that Rome was a holy city. But both of his epistles and the historical record in Acts are silent about this important matter. Silence is not golden; in this case, it speaks volumes. We can venture a good guess about why Peter never mentions his bishopric in the holy city of Rome. He was never there, was never a bishop, and was never buried there.

Not only is Jerusalem called a holy city in the Bible several times, but it is also called the holy hill, the holy place, the holy habitation, and Mt. Zion. It is surprising how many times it is called the holy mountain (Isaiah 56:7 and Zechariah 8:3). Rome is never mentioned as a holy city.

The apostle Paul wanted to visit Rome, he says, to teach them the gospel. But he never called Rome the holy city or mentioned meeting Peter there. Of special interest to the Jewish people, Jerusalem will someday be "trampled underfoot by the Gentiles" (Luke 21:24).

This will take place at some point in the future, during the seven-year period known in the Bible as the Tribulation (Matthew 24:21). Though Jerusalem will be destroyed, God will replace it with the New Jerusalem (Revelation 3:12, 21:2), which will be far superior to the old city. The replacing will occur with Jesus Christ's Second Coming to Earth. God will reestablish David's throne and will place His Son, Jesus, on it, and he will rule Israel and the world as the King of kings and the Lord of lords.

When Christ returns to Earth, everything will undergo a change. There will be a new heaven and Earth. The old heaven and Earth will perish in the same sense that the Earth of Noah's day perished. *Perish* does not necessarily mean "cease to exist," but rather, to undergo huge changes. The desert will blossom as a rose; mountains and valleys will undergo topographical changes. The devastation of the earth, caused by the events of the Tribulation, will be cleaned up, refreshed, and the land made livable again. Who knows what will happen to Rome? It likely will cease to be the center of any religion.

Many biblical scholars believe that the old Roman Empire will be revived with Rome as the center of its government. If this is true, it won't last long—at least, no longer than the seven years of the Tribulation. The center of government will reside in Jerusalem after the Tribulation years.

The true holy city in the Bible is Jerusalem, the city of David. David was the first king of Israel from the tribe of Judah. He was responsible for making Jerusalem the royal residence of Jewish kings. David was buried either there or in Bethlehem (1 Kings 2:10). In God's sight, Jerusalem is the center of Earth. All directions in the Bible are either north, south, east, or west of Jerusalem.

Does it matter what one believes about what is holy? It certainly matters if a person's allegiance is to the wrong holy city, and that city is headed to oblivion. Misplaced allegiances serve no good purpose at all. The church, called the body of Christ in the Bible, has no holy city here on Earth. The destiny of the church is the heavens, where it will reside forever in the heavenly kingdom (2 Timothy 4:18).

CHAPTER 15
SIN

AMONG THE MANY things that are clear in the Bible is that God is offended by sin, and that His domain in the heavens has no place for it. On Earth, it is an ever-present reality.

What is sin? Let's go to the expert on the matter, let God say what sin is, and then we can be sure we have the right answer. The Lord inspired John to write, "All wrongdoing is sin" (1 John 5:17). Wrongdoing covers a lot of ground. Solomon helps us by naming "haughty eyes and a proud heart" in Proverbs 21:4. Again, he identifies "the scheme of a fool" and "the scoffer" as an abomination to God in Proverbs 24:9.

Paul says, "Whatever is not from faith is sin" in Romans 14:23. Faith comes to us from the Bible; we cannot generate it from within ourselves. Therefore, whatsoever is not of faith is the rejection of God's Word. John says, "Sin is lawlessness" (1 John 3:4). It is disobedience to God's laws. Romans makes it plain and clear: "All have sinned and are deprived of the glory of God" (Romans 3:23). Sin is a serious problem for mankind, and something needs to be done about it. No one can enter God's presence in heaven with sin charged against his or her account.

Just how serious is the sin problem? Man is incapable of correcting the problem. He does not have the power, the knowledge, or the means to fix it. God, in His infinite knowledge, not only knows all about the problem; He has the perfect solution to it. God knows we are helpless and without hope, unable to cure ourselves of sin, and have no remedy when we are left to ourselves. In His mercy and grace, God has fixed the problem for us. He did for us what we could not do for ourselves. He sent into the world His only begotten Son for the express purpose of dying on the cross at Calvary and paying "the wages of sin" for us (Romans 6:23). He redeemed us, reconciled us to Himself, and forgave us; He justified us, sanctified us, and washed us clean in His sight. Jesus paid it all.

Based on the saving work of Jesus Christ, God offered the gift of everlasting life, which makes it possible to enter His glorious presence when we die. The offer of salvation as a gift puts the responsibility on us to respond to His offer and receive it. The choice is ours. He will save us from a never-ending hell and from the lake of fire if we will do one thing: believe in and receive the Lord, Jesus Christ, as our Savior. In Acts 16, when the Philippian jail warden asked Paul and Silas how he could be saved from hell, their answer was, "Believe in the Lord Jesus and you [if you believe] and your household [if they believe] will be saved" (Acts 16:31). So, there it is; and that's it! So easy and simple.

What does it mean to believe in the Lord, Jesus Christ? It means to believe what the Bible says about Him and to trust in everything God has done through His Son to make our salvation possible. The person who receives the Lord as his or her own personal Savior will be immediately blessed by God with salvation that will last for eternity. The newly saved sinner becomes a child of God and will never be disowned. Salvation is never referred to as temporary, but rather, as everlasting. It's life for eternity.

A major problem for humanity is that we want to deal with problems in our own way, the sin problem included. We don't want to believe what the Bible teaches about sin, so we do what religion does so well: we add to what the Bible says. This results in contradictions and misapplications. It produces a theology that nobody can understand. The Bible says, "Trust in the Lord with all your heart; on your own intelligence do not rely" Proverbs 3:5. We trust in the Lord, who speaks to us through the scriptures. Without the guidance of God's Word, we lean on our own understanding.

The Catholic Church teaches that we pay, to some degree, for our own sins. They have a sacrament called *penance* by which the sins committed after baptism are forgiven through the absolution of a priest. Penance raises the soul from death to supernatural life. It provides forgiveness of sins and remission of eternal punishment (*Baltimore Catechism*, lesson twenty-nine). The sacrament of baptism also takes away all sin (lesson thirty-one). All Catholics are urged to confess their sins at least once a year (lesson twenty-two).

The statements from the *Baltimore Catechism* contradict the scriptures. The Church teaches that penance and baptism take away sins. The Bible, which is God's Word, teaches that sins are washed away in their entirety by the shed blood of Jesus Christ (Ephesians 1:7). Nowhere does the Bible limit the power of Christ's blood to anything less than completely washing away a person's sin. We do not need penance and baptism to take away sin, and those things do not have the power to do so. When a sinner receives Christ as his or her Savior, he or she is completely forgiven on the spot and does not need a priest to be absolved. The traditional teachings of the Catholic Church are misleading and will lead a person into eternity forever separated from God and heaven.

Do Christians sin? They do, and their sins are covered by the blood. But we must not make the mistake here of thinking that there is no consequence for the sins we commit as Christians. There is a natural, unpleasant result from sin. Immorality is a sin soundly condemned in the Bible. If a person lives an immoral life, whether that person is a Christian or not, this can result in serious infections like venereal disease or HIV. It can cause devastating results to personal relationships. It can bring about embarrassment, loss of work, and many other consequences. Drunkenness is condemned in the Bible and is a sin. If a person drinks to excess, drives a car, and involves him- or herself in a serious accident—perhaps with fatalities—then that is a natural consequence to sin. These outcomes are not judgments from God. He does not cause these results; neither does He stop them from happening.

God's judgment is yet in the future. When a person dies in sin, that person will appear before the great white throne mentioned in Revelation 20:11. From there, he or she will be cast into the pool of fire (Revelation 20:10–15), where that person will dwell forever in torment, pain, and darkness, forever forgotten by loved ones in heaven and by God.

God can forget perfectly if He so desires, and He can cause those in heaven to forget things that would sadden them. The *Baltimore Catechism* never says a word about the great white throne or the lake of fire. Omitting these warnings of future judgment is very serious. Having humanity pay for its own sins in any degree is a serious blunder that will definitely cost a sinner his or her salvation. Humans cannot save or help save themselves.

Look at what the Bible says: "She will bear a son and you are to name him Jesus, because he will save his people from their sins" (Matthew 1:21). "But if we walk in the light, as he is in the light, then we have fellowship with one another, and the blood of his Son Jesus cleanses us from all sin" (1 John 1:7). When the Bible says, "from all sin," why isn't that enough? How much sin is left for humans to pay for by baptism, penance, Purgatory, absolutions, and so on, after *all* sin has been paid for? It seems clear that something is terribly wrong with the teachings in the catechism. Does it matter what we believe?

Israel had a sacrificial system, established by God, in which the sins of the Jews were dealt with. Their sins were only atoned for— that is, they were covered but not taken away. It was a temporary arrangement until Christ could come into the world and die on the cross. He became the final sacrifice for the sins of Israel. His sacrifice was then made available to the whole world, offering cleansing from all sin to those who would believe in Him. A well-known verse, in John 3:16, says, "For God so loved the world that he gave his only Son, so that everyone who believes in him might not perish but have eternal life." Refusal to believe in Him means that a person rejects the love of God. There is no substitute for the Lamb of God, who takes away the sin of the world. All the labor of people's hands, all their well-meant intentions, all their vows and prayers, good works, financial contributions, church attendance, confessions, and so on, will not contribute one thing toward their salvation. Partial belief in Jesus will not save a soul.

How does Israel fit into God's program for today? The Jews have no special place at this point in history. God has placed upon them a spiritual slumber so that the nation cannot see or hear the truth. An individual Jew can be saved, but the nation cannot until it has suffered through the Tribulation. That's what they get for nonstop rejection of God's offer to save them and for the awful rejection of their Messiah; they demanded that Christ be crucified. Then the Jews proceeded to persecute the Lord's disciples and all who believed in Him. Enough is enough! According to Romans 11, God has cast Israel aside. God's rejection of the Jews is temporary, however; He will reclaim them as His people once again at Christ's Second Coming.

If we set aside the Catechism, what is left?

1. We have only the Bible, which says we are sinners.
2. We have the worldwide testimony of humanity, the universal recognition of sin. All have sinned.
3. We have the witness of our conscience. We know we have sinned against God.

John's book of Revelation tells us that, at some point in the future, God will judge sinners who preferred religion over His plan of salvation.

> Next I saw a large white throne and the one who was sitting on it. The earth and the sky fled from his presence and there was no place for them. I saw the dead, the great and the lowly, standing before the throne, and scrolls were opened. Then another scroll was opened, the book of life. The dead were judged according to their deeds, by what was written in the scrolls. The sea gave up its dead; then Death and Hades gave up their dead. All the dead were judged according to their deeds. Then Death and Hades were thrown into the pool of fire. [The pool of fire is the second death.] Anyone whose name was not found written in the book of life was thrown into the pool of fire. (Revelation 20:11–14)

Only sinners will be present at this judgment throne. They will be there because they choose not to believe in and receive God's simple plan of salvation. Many of them will be very religious during their lifetimes, but being religious does not save their souls. They will be present before the judge without excuse or recourse. They can blame whomever they want, but that will not help. Every person is responsible for his or her own choices that are made during life on Earth.

Religions all over the world are systems that humans have invented that involve good works of all kinds and forms. Christianity is different. It is not a religion. It is a belief system that involves trusting the Bible alone to teach us God's way to be saved—which means believing in the Lord, Jesus Christ, to save us alone. The apostle Paul makes it as clear as can be in Ephesians 2:8–9, "For by grace you have been saved through faith, and this is not from you, it is the gift of God. It is not from works, so no one may boast."

One way that humans deal with sin is to apply labels. Thus, we read in the catechisms that there are venial sins and mortal sins, actual sins, original sins, and more. Actual sins are those that are intentional, accompanied by sins of omission, grievous sins, original sin, formal sin, material sin, and capital sin. Why use all these labels that are not found in the Bible? They say that, in God's eyes, some sins are not as bad as others, and some are too bad to be forgiven. What is the unforgiveable sin mentioned in Luke 12:10?

After Christ was crucified, risen, and ascended into heaven, the Holy Spirit was given to empower the twelve apostles to perform supernatural deeds. These miracles were necessary to prove that God was with them and that they truly were servants of God. If the Holy Spirit–empowered ministry was rejected, then there was no divine witness of the Godhead left in the world. At that time, the Bible was not yet completed.

In the Old Testament, God, the Father, was rejected—first by the families with which humanity had its beginnings, and then by Israel. In the four gospels of the New Testament, God, the Son, was rejected by the nation of Israel, the people of God. In Acts, God, the Holy Spirit, was rejected when the Jews stood steadfast in their rejection by refusing to believe the gospel that the apostles preached. That was the unforgivable sin.

People dislike recognizing how sinful they are. They think better of themselves and downplay their sins, thinking they are not bad enough to damn their souls to hell, with the exception of the worst kinds of sins. Comedians make jokes about sin. They often think sin is funny. They have no fear of a God of love and scoff at the penalty for sin. There's nothing new about that.

God does not think sin is funny; it cost Him His only Son. He had to pay for our sins by sending His Son into the world to pay our debts. Some refer to our sins as being "little white things," or "light matters" that God does not take notice of; they do not believe these are worthy of His attention. But sin is sin, and it is very offensive to God. Not one goes unnoticed, no matter what degree it is.

If we go to the ultimate authority on sin, namely the triune Godhead, we find that He has spoken about it in His Word. We cannot trust people's philosophies or religions. God's Word is the first and only reliable guide. "Therefore, just as through one person sin entered the world, and through sin, death, and thus death came to all, inasmuch as all sinned" (Romans 5:12).

We are spiritually dead until we receive Christ as our Savior. "In my heart I treasure your promise, that I might not sin against you" (Psalm 119:11). It has been said that either God's Word will direct us away from sin, or sin will direct us away from God's Word. "But as for cowards, the unfaithful, the depraved, murderers, the unchaste, sorcerers, idol-worshipers, and deceivers of every sort, their lot is in the burning pool of fire and sulfur, which is the second death" (Revelation 21:8). This is the everlasting state of the sinner who rejects God's gracious plan and offer of salvation. God's judgment is final. Does it matter what a person believes about sin? Where one will spend eternity depends on what is believed now.

CHAPTER 16
IDOLATRY, IMAGES, STATUES, AND RELICS

ONE OF THE many differences between fundamental Protestant theology and Catholicism is the number of statues and images honored by Catholics. Protestants ask, what is the difference between an image and an idol? Does anyone really believe that saints are honored by statues and images? Obviously, people do believe it.

Where in the Bible does it say that Mary or the saints were honored with statues? Most people agree that a statue or an image cannot see, hear, think, or know anything; these have no life in them. Do they represent spirit beings of any kind? Does it make a difference if the image is carved, graven, formed in a mold, painted on a canvas, or made of stained glass?

In view of the use and purpose of images and statues, how can this practice be justified when the Bible forbids it in Exodus 20? God instructed Moses to forbid the Israelites from making images. "You shall not make for yourself an idol or a likeness of *anything* in the heavens above or on the earth below or in the waters beneath the earth. You shall not bow down before them or serve them" (Exodus 20:4–5, emphasis mine). The apostle Paul commends the Thessalonians, "For they themselves openly declare about us what sort of reception we had among you, and how you turned to God from idols to serve the living and true God" (1 Thessalonians 1:9). Are there exceptions to God's commands? Can God, Jesus, Mary, or the saints be any better pleased if we entertain idols and images, than if they are not worshipped?

One thing seems clear: God does not want to be represented by human-made things as the Father, Son, or Holy Spirit. God, the Father, and the Holy Spirit are invisible spirit beings (John 4:24) and cannot be visibly represented. Only Jesus Christ, the Son of God, has been seen by humans. Something that is invisible, like a spirit, can hardly be represented in a concrete form; neither can it set forth any truth.

A leading reason why humans make images is that we feel the need to see something. "Seeing is believing," or so the saying goes. This is not necessarily true. The Pharisees and scribes saw the miracles of Jesus, and it did not make believers out of them. They ascribed Jesus's miracles to Beelzebub. But the Bible says that we do not walk by sight; we walk by faith (2 Corinthians 5:7). Religion loves to see things. In the Bible, images were a source of income for those who made them, as was the case in Acts 19. Paul and Silas had entered Ephesus and had successfully preached the gospel. So great was the impact of the apostles' preaching that many dedicated, deeply religious Ephesians abandoned the worship of the goddess Diana to believe in Jesus Christ. This caused the guild of silversmiths, who made statues of Diana and her temple, to rise up against the apostles because the silversmiths were losing money from their trade. Making idols was a great money-maker. Are relics, images, statues, idols, and paintings big money-makers today?

The divine attributes, characteristics, and personality traits of the Godhead cannot be adequately represented by the work of humans' hands. In fact, they may be misleading, bringing God down to humankind's level. We do not find in the Bible that the heavenly saints were to be honored by images and statues or by any other means. The attention and honor given to such things is nothing short of worship and is therefore idolatry. Protestants do not see any difference between honor and worship.

One of the ways in which the saints in heaven are honored is "by showing respect to their relics and images" (*Catechism*, lesson 17, number 216). Number 219 also says, "We honor relics because they are the bodies of the saints or objects connected with the saints of the Lord." What scripture is used to support this practice? Second Kings 13:20–21, which says, "And so Elisha died and was buried. At that time of year, bands of Moabites used to raid the land. Once some people were burying a man, when suddenly they saw such a raiding band. So they cast the man into the grave of Elisha, and everyone went off. But when the man came in contact with the bones of Elisha, he came back to life, and got to his feet." These are the verses used to support the honoring of relics. It is an extremely far stretch to come to such a conclusion. It is impossible to find support for honoring relics from this passage of scripture.

Deuteronomy is so clear:

> Because you saw no form at all on the day the Lord spoke to you at Horeb from the midst of the fire, be strictly on your guard not to act corruptly by fashioning an idol for yourselves to represent any figure, whether it be the form of a man or of a woman, the form of any animal on earth, the form of any bird that flies in the sky, the form of anything that crawls on the ground, or the form of any fish in the waters under the earth. And when you look up to the heavens and behold the sun or the moon or the stars, the whole heavenly host, do not be led astray by bowing down to them and serving them. Deuteronomy 4:15–19

There is nothing vague about Moses's instructions. These verses condemn worship, honor, and veneration of images of any kind.

The Catholic Church teaches in the *Baltimore Catechism*, lesson 17, number 220 and 221, that it is wrong to make images, statues, and paintings of Christ and the saints when they promote false worship. But it is no more wrong to show respect to them than it is to show respect for our family members. Catholics do not actually pray to statues, relics, pictures, images, or crucifixes; instead, they pray to those whom these things represent. They know that the thousands of statues of Mary are lifeless but represent a real, living person to whom they pray without ceasing. They do not worship or adore these in the same way that they do God—or so they say, but non-Catholics are not convinced.

Years ago, when some excavation work was being done in St. Peter's Cathedral in Rome, bones were discovered. The discovery was made public, and the Church said they were almost proven to be St. Peter's bones. They did not say how this was almost proven, but it appears that it was a desperate attempt to place the Lord's apostle in Rome before his death. There is also a claim to have a lock of Mary's hair and a container of milk from her breast. The Church has also claimed that they have what are believed to be the actual nails that were used in Jesus's crucifixion. It has been thought that they have produced enough of these nails worldwide to build the Eiffel Tower. The Catholic Church is known for the relics they say are those deserving of their respect.

Why do Protestants reject statues, images, relics, beads, crucifixes, and many other things as objects of "spiritual respect"? Some principles stated in the Bible are interdispensational, meaning it does not matter where in history one lives; the principles are always applicable. Moses gave Israel God's law in Exodus, forbidding the making and observing of such things, including paintings, engravings, and other forms of artwork—and that law is still on the books today.

Who has the right to remove or change what the Bible says? In Mosaic law, the law was and still is, "You shall not make for yourselves an idol or likeness of anything" (Exodus 20:4) because

God understands the making of such things to be a form of worship. He thinks differently than humans do. "You shall not bow down before them or serve them" (Exodus 20:5). Did the Ephesians in Acts 19 believe that the statue of Diana was alive and that she could see and hear? Of course not! The statue represented a spirit being whom they considered a goddess, and the respect given to it was considered worship.

God will not share. He alone must receive all worship, honor, and respect. To make images and the like is an active form of rebellion and wickedness. The Latin word for adore is *adoro,* a compound word, meaning "to pray to a superior being." Those who adore hope to be rewarded for their attention. To adore can take such forms as crossing oneself, tipping the hat, bowing, or simply having a reverential thought.

Does it matter what we believe about relics, statues, images, pictures, or representations of any kind with respect to the Godhead or the saints? According to the Bible, it matters to God. According to tradition and religion, it is acceptable. We already know what God thinks. Which way is right? Which way is most acceptable in God's eyes? It mattered to the Ephesians and the Thessalonians. Why shouldn't it matter to us?

CHAPTER 17
THE APOSTLE PAUL

ACCORDING TO THE Bible, Simon Peter was the apostle to Israel. We know this because it says in Matthew 10:6, "Go rather to the lost sheep of the house of Israel." This was the Lord's commission to Peter and the eleven apostles. They had no ministry to the Gentiles. The apostle who God raised up to go to the Gentiles was Paul. He said to the church in Rome, "Now I am speaking to you Gentiles, inasmuch then as I am the apostle to the Gentiles, I glory in my ministry" (Romans 11:13).

As far as the record shows, these commissions were never changed or altered. As late as Acts 15, the twelve apostles were still going to the circumcision nation, Israel. Acts 15 gives the historical account of the church conference held in Jerusalem to determine whether Paul's ministry was legitimate. The results of the conference are summarized in Galatians 2:9, where we have the conclusion of the meeting: "And when they [the conference leaders] recognized the grace [gospel of grace] bestowed upon me [Paul], James and Cephas [Peter] and John, who were reputed to be pillars, gave me and Barnabas their right hands of partnership, that we [Paul and Barnabas] should go to the Gentiles and they [the twelve] should go to the circumcision [the nation of Israel]." Paul wrote his epistle to the Galatian Christians years after he was converted on the Damascus road.

The ministries of the twelve apostles and the apostle Paul must be separated from each other because they were different ministries. If the two ministries are not rightly divided, confusion and wrong application of scripture will surely result. This has happened to the Catholic Church, resulting in the thinking that Peter went to Rome and was the first bishop and pope of the Church. The NABRE does not support this conclusion.

Consider Paul's words in 1 Corinthians 3:10–11. "According to the grace of God [gospel of grace] given to me, like a wise master builder I laid the foundation and another is building upon it. But each one must be careful how he builds upon it. For no one can lay a foundation other than the one that is there, namely, Jesus Christ." The church is not and cannot be built on Peter; it is built on the Lord, Jesus Christ, and Paul laid the foundation for it.

Because Paul was led by the Lord to establish the church that he called the body of Christ, Paul then instructs believers several times to imitate him—namely, to follow his teachings of the gospel of grace. "Be imitators of me, as I am of Christ" (1 Corinthians 11:1). He said the same thing earlier in the epistle: "Therefore, I urge you, be imitators of me" (1 Corinthians 4:16). In Philippians, Paul says, "Join with others in being imitators of me" (Philippians 3:17). Paul preached the gospel that he learned from the Lord as it says in Galatians 1, and he urges others to follow him in the propagation of the gospel of the message of grace. In fact, when he says *imitate*, he uses the imperative mood, which, in Greek, is the mood of command.

After reading through the *Baltimore Catechism* number 3, from numbers 1 to 499, one cannot find a mention of Paul as the apostle to the Gentiles. There are many quotes in the catechism from his epistles, especially in the section from 443 to 499, but not an explanation about Paul's unique ministry.

Peter never urges anyone to imitate him. Matthew 10:6 records the Lord's commission to the twelve disciples, who also were called apostles, in which He named Peter as the leader and limited their ministry to "the lost sheep of the house of Israel." This commission never changed during the earthly ministry of the twelve.

How did the ministries of Peter and Paul differ from each other? Peter taught the mysteries of the kingdom of heaven. Paul taught the mysteries of the church, the body of Christ. During Peter's ministry, God had no program for the Gentiles. God's attention was toward the Jews alone. Beginning with Paul, God turns His attention back to the Gentiles and the whole world (Acts 13:46, 18:6). The Gentiles were cast aside when God called Abraham out of Chaldea. Israel was set aside when God called Paul (Romans 11:11–15).

Peter was a dedicated keeper of the Mosaic law, which explains why he hesitated to go to the house of Cornelius in Acts 10. Paul did not keep the Mosaic law but declared that the law ended (Romans 6:14–15; Galatians 5:18). The law ended with the casting aside of Israel in Romans 11. Since the law was given to Israel, and Israel was cast aside, there was no more need for the law.

Peter looked forward to the Second Coming of Christ to restore Israel's lost kingdom. Paul looked forward to the appearing of Jesus Christ (often called the Rapture), when Christ will come back in the clouds of heaven and take the body of Christ to heaven, thus ending the church age (1 Thessalonians 4:13–18).

Peter knew the nation of Israel would pass through the Tribulation and that it would end with the Second Coming. Paul knew the body of Christ would not pass through the Tribulation but would be delivered from its wrath by the Lord's appearance before the Tribulation upon Israel commences (1 Thessalonians 1:10).

Peter observed the Sabbath, worshipped at the temple in Jerusalem at prayer time, baptized believers, and practiced circumcision. Paul was not a Sabbath keeper, worshipped the Lord wherever he was, said he was not sent to baptize, and that circumcision meant nothing anymore (Galatians 6:15; 1 Corinthians 1:17).

Peter performed numerous miracles, and Paul duplicated each one. The difference was that miracles were used to validate the ministry of the twelve and were in full force until Israel was set aside. Paul performed miracles until the scriptures were completed, and then they ceased. His miracles validated his ministry, especially to the Jews who walk by sight. The church, the body of Christ, walks by faith.

When Peter ministered, he was accompanied by eleven other apostles. Twelve apostles were necessary because there will be twelve thrones reserved in the kingdom age for them. When Paul ministered, no other apostles were necessary; he was the only one called by the Lord to minister to the world—Jews and Gentiles alike. In a sense, he worked alone, but in another sense, he had many coworkers—some of whom are referred to as apostles.

Peter was never a priest, but somehow, according to the Church, he became the forerunner of a long line of priests—none of whom could trace their ancestry back to Levi, the father of Israel's priestly family. The Catholic priests are not Jews. Paul was not a priest and never included or relied on priests to carry on the ministry. Instead, he spoke to those who became pastors and teachers. The bishops he mentions were never priests.

From the beginning of creation, God has been the God of all grace, but, through the early ages of the Gentiles and the nation of Israel, works were always required. Without works, faith was dead (James 2:20). Peter knew that God dealt with Israel by grace but not apart from the works of the law. Paul knew the exact opposite. He preached in Ephesians 2:8–9 and Titus 3:5 that we are saved by grace through faith, apart from works of righteousness.

During the age in which Peter ministered, converts to Judaism from among the Gentiles were called *proselytes*. During Paul's ministry, there were no proselytes because nobody was being converted to Judaism. Instead, they were being saved from the wages of sin and added to the church, the body of Christ as members.

There are more differences, but enough have been given to

make the point. Some differences discussed in this text are without scriptural references, but be assured, they are completely scriptural. They are not the traditional teachings of fundamental Protestants, but rather, they are recorded in the Bible for our learning. Learning how to rightly divide the Bible the way that God has divided it will save us from error and heresy. Our aim is to make the same divisions that God makes and to rightly apply them to us.

In view of the Lord's commands, does it matter who we follow? Will we follow Peter or Paul? Will we live under the Mosaic law or under grace, free from the law?

CHAPTER 18
SUMMARY

CARL MARX HAD one thing right: "Religion is the opiate of the people." It has been shown in the opening chapter of this book that many people in the Bible who were "deeply religious" perished in their sins. They thought that religion was the way to God. The religions of the world are manmade worship systems, and not one of them is acceptable to God. Only Christianity offers God's perfect and complete plan of salvation to lost sinners. When it comes to a belief system, it certainly matters what a person believes. One's eternal destiny depends on it.

Tradition cannot and should not be trusted as being God's Word. It is humanity's word, and it victimizes its followers. It sounds spiritual and good, and it is a way that "seems right, but the end of it leads to death" (Proverbs 16:25). It will matter for all eternity to trust in something that people claim is God's Word but is not.

Many things the Catholic Church believes and teaches about Mary are traditional doctrines, which means they are not scriptural. In fact, the Bible denies that Mary has any part in people's salvation or that she can intercede in any way for us. She does not have the power to hear or answer prayers.

What is believed about Simon Peter is clearly denied by the Bible. He was the apostle to Israel, never to the Gentiles, and he was not the rock on which the church was built. The Lord, Jesus Christ, is the rock. Peter was never in Rome; neither was he the first bishop of the Church or the first in a long line of popes.

"Call no man Father" in Matthew 23:9 seems clear enough. We have one heavenly Father and one earthly biological father. We also have spiritual fathers. A Holy Father is a person who has taken this title for himself. Saying he is the Holy Father does not make it so. The head of the church is the Lord, Jesus Christ, alone.

The priesthood of the Catholic Church does not resemble the priesthood of Israel. No Catholic priests are of the tribe of Levi, can forgive sins, or were ever given spiritual authority over the Church. The Church has pastors and teachers, bishops, and elders who are servants and not lords.

The doctrine of transubstantiation is as false as can be. The wine and wafer never change into anything. The consumption of human flesh and blood is revolting and forbidden by God, and there is reason to believe that many Catholics do not believe the wafer and wine change into the flesh and blood of Christ.

The sacrifice of the mass is unnecessary. Christ died once and ascended into heaven, where He is now seated at the right hand of the Father, waiting for the appointed time when He will return in the clouds to call the church, the body of Christ, out of this world. After the Tribulation—that is, the outpouring of God's wrath—Christ will return to Earth to establish His kingdom, regather Israel, sit on David's throne, and rule as King of kings and Lord of lords.

In the Bible, the church is called the body of Christ. Its members are those who have received Jesus Christ as their own personal Savior. Membership does not require membership in any religious church on Earth or on being baptized, confirmed, or having any kind of traditional ceremonies. One only needs to believe in Christ to be saved.

Baptism is one of many misunderstood doctrines in the Bible. The reason for this is that the Bible is not studied to see if what it teaches about baptism is true. Of the twelve baptisms mentioned in the Bible, the only necessary baptism for the church is that of the Holy Spirit, who baptizes a new believer into the body of Christ when the person first believes in Christ for salvation. No water is involved. When a person is saved, that person is baptized without water into the body of Christ by the Holy Spirit.

The Bible is the sole authority for the truth. Tradition does not have equal authority with the Bible and is not inspired by God. When a person receives Christ as his or her Savior, he or she immediately becomes a saint. The Church does not decide this based on merits or spiritual deeds. A person may not look like a saint or act like one, but this does not mean he or she is not a saint.

When a person dies, his or her soul goes somewhere. If the person is a believer in Christ, the soul goes to heaven. The person enters into the presence of the Lord, where they remain together for eternity. The Bible does not mention a place called Purgatory, where the deceased go to pay for their unforgiven sins. A believer's sins are completely forgiven. If a person dies without receiving Christ as his or her Savior, the person will go to hell to await the final judgment of the great white throne. There is no escape from hell. The decision of where one will spend eternity is made while living, and once a person dies, death finalizes that decision. It can never be changed.

The only holy city mentioned in the Bible is Jerusalem. All other cities that are called holy cities are inventions of religions, and the Lord does not recognize them. They will be destroyed during the Tribulation, and the true holy city of Jerusalem will remain and will be restored for the millennial reign of Christ. It will be the seat of world government, and Rome will be destroyed.

Sin offends God. There is no such thing as venial or mortal sin. All sins are alike to God. Some sins are more heinous than others, but, in the end, they all are dealt with alike. When Christ died for sinners, all sins were paid for, in full, and God offers salvation to all who believe in the finished work of Jesus Christ. If a person never receives Christ as his or her Savior, then that person goes to hell as an unbeliever, never having appropriated God's forgiveness.

There is no need for images, statues, relics, and other forms of human-made objects to remind one of the triune Godhead, Mary, or deceased saints. If we read the Bible, all we need to remind us of God and the Lord, Jesus Christ, is written there for us. Read the Bible and forget the things people make that have no power to do what the Bible can do for us. They have the power to distort the truth and misrepresent God and His Son and should be discarded and avoided.

Finally, when we read through the *Baltimore Catechism*, we must ask, where is Paul? The Catholic Church's recognition of Paul as the apostle to the world, the Jew and the Gentile alike, is like a soap bubble that appears and quickly disappears.

God loves every Roman Catholic ever born, with a love that cannot be greater. It is maximum love, love in its purest form, and it is all-sufficient. Every Catholic can be saved and assured of it by receiving Jesus Christ as his or her only Savior to the total exclusion of all other persons or things that claim to save. There is no age or gender limit. Salvation never depends on wealth, power, popularity, or personal appearance. God is not impressed with any of the things that so impress humanity.

Believe in the Lord, Jesus Christ, and be saved (Acts 16:31–32). This is what matters, both now and for all eternity.

BIBLIOGRAPHY

Berry, George Ricker, The Interlinear Greek-English New Testament, Zondervan Publishing House, Grand Rapids, MI, 1977.

Breten, Sir Lancelot C. L. The Septuagent with the Apocraphy Greek and English, Regency Reference Library, Samuel Bagster & Son, London, England, 1851.

Bruce, F. F., J. I. Packer, R. V. G. Tasker, and D. J. Wiseman Douglas, The New Bible Dictionary, W. F. Eerdman's Publishing, Grand Rapids, MI, 1073.

Bullinger, E. W., Figures of Speech, Baker Book House, Grand Rapids, MI, 1981.

Crabb, George, Crabb's English Synonyms, London, England, Rutledge and Kegan Paul, 1966.

Daana, Harvey Eugene, and Julius R. Mantey, A Manual Grammar of the Greek New Testament, Macmillan, New York, New York, 1955.

Davis, John D., A Dictionary of the Bible, The Westminster Press, Philadelphia, PA, 1942.

Fredericksen, John, God's Meaning in Matthew, Berean Bible Society, Germantown, WI, 2916.

Ginder, Rev. Richard, C. I. S. Extension Course based on the Confraternity of Christian Doctrine, revised edition of the Baltimore Catechism No. 3, New York, New York, 1841.

Halley, Henry H., Halley's Handbook of the Bible, 24th edition, Zondervan Publishing House, Grand Rapids, MI, 1065.

Pardington, George, Outline Studies in Christian Doctrine, Christian Publications, Inc., Harrisburg, PA, 1926.

Stam, C. S., The Lord's Supper, Berean Bible Society, Chicago, IL, 1981.

Strong, James, Strong's Exhaustive Concordance of the Bible, Thomas Nelson, Nashville, TN., 1982.

Unger, Merrill F., Unger's Bible Dictionary, Moody Press, Chicago, IL, 1977.

Webster, Noah, Jean L. McKechnie, Wenster's New Twentieth Century Dictionary of the English Language, The World Publishing Company, New York, NY, 1957.

Wigram, George V., G. K. The Englishman's Greek Concordance of the New Testament, Zondervan Publishing House, Grand Rapids, MI, 1976.

Printed in the United States
by Baker & Taylor Publisher Services